Canyon Country

OFF-ROAD VEHICLE TRAILS
Island Area
by
F. A. Barnes

**An illustrated guide to the
backcountry roads and off-road
vehicle trails in one area of
southeastern Utah's canyon country**

1988
Canyon Country Publications

This book is the FOURTH in a series
of practical guides to travel and recreation
in the scenic Colorado Plateau region of the
Four Corners States

PRINTING HISTORY
First published in 1978
by Wasatch Publishers, Salt Lake City

Completely updated in 1988 and
reprinted by Canyon Country Publications
in larger format with
additional illustrations

Artwork by Kathy Nunley

Copyright 1988
Canyon Country Publications
P. O. Box 963
Moab, Utah 84532

ISBN 0-9614586-6-6
LCN 88-070881

CONTENTS

AREA MAP . . . . Inside front cover

INTRODUCTION
    Guidebook Series 5
    Area Covered By This Book 5
    Supplementary Information 5
    Area Terrain 5
    Maps 7
    Navigation 7
    Base Camps 8
    Seasons 8
    Access Roads 9
    Trail Description Format 11
    Area Notes 13

TRAIL SEGMENTS
    Alphabetical Listing 14
    Trail Descriptions . . . . .15 through 73

SUGGESTED MULTI-SEGMENT ROUTES
    Listing 75
    Route Descriptions . . . . .75 through 78

AUTHOR'S FAVORITE TRAILS 79

FURTHER READING . . . . .80 and
                                       inside back cover

White Rim trail, Canyonlands National Park

INTRODUCTION

GUIDEBOOK SERIES

This is one of a series of practical guidebooks, each one listing and describing the off-road vehicle trails within one or more distinct areas of the canyon country of southeastern Utah. Each of these areas is defined by a combination of manmade boundaries, such as highways, and natural barriers that bar travel by off-road vehicle, such as rivers.

AREA COVERED BY THIS BOOK

This book covers the large area west of Moab, Utah, defined by Interstate 70 on the north, the Green River on the west and U.S. 191 and the Colorado River on the east, and includes the Island-in-the-Sky district of Canyonlands National Park. A map elsewhere in this book shows these boundaries, and the entire area has been named "Island Area" for the purposes of this book.

This book lists and describes all of the backcountry access roads into the area defined, and most of the major off-road vehicle trail segments there, but is not intended to be comprehensive. Those who have explored the trails in this book will by then be able to continue their explorations of this area without further guidance.

SUPPLEMENTARY INFORMATION

Other guidebooks in the *Canyon Country* series contain supplementary information concerning perimeter and access roads, natural and human history, hiking, mountain biking, camping, archeology, other modes of exploration, facilities, supplies and services, and the parks in this area.

AREA TERRAIN

The Island Area in general is high, arid to semi-arid desert, broken by huge sandstone outcroppings and buttes, and slashed by hundreds of shallow washes, deeper canyons and great, sheer-walled gorges. The wide variety of geologic formations found in the area provide color, diversity of shape in land forms, and variations in trail surfaces. The area can be divided into four distinct kinds of terrain, each with its own type of scenic beauty and special highlights.

The northeastern half of the northern third of the area is relatively flat, open country dominated by colorless seabottom shale interspersed with alluvial sand and gravel, dune sand and some outcroppings of older sandstone deposits. This area may be of some interest to collectors seeking sealife and other fossils, but contains few trails of interest to most off-road explorers.

The southwestern half of this northern third of the area is more colorful, offers good hunting for mineral collectors, and has a number of trails worth exploring, but does not contain the kind of spectacular scenery that dominates the southern two-thirds of the area.

The central portion of the Island Area is broad, open sand flats studded with massive domes, mesas and ridges of red-hued, monolithic sandstone. This high desert also contains several large areas dominated by eroded white sandstone and sand dunes, and is deeply cut by a complex series of huge canyons that radiate in all directions from a promontory called The Knoll.

These canyons all eventually join the great gorges of the Green and Colorado rivers. As these gorges converge to their confluence within the heart of Canyonlands National Park, the plateauland narrows to become the long, branching, sheer-walled peninsula called Island-in-the-Sky. Dead Horse Point is another such peninsula.

The fourth type of terrain in the Island Area is found below the high Island-in-the-Sky and adjoining plateau country, on an intermediate level that is still above the Colorado and Green Rivers. The unusual white sandstone formation that is the foundation of this immense benchland slopes gradually upward from north to south. It is dominated on one side by the sheer red cliffs and great talus slopes of Island-in-the-Sky and associated highlands. Below the benchland, weirdly eroded, dark red sandstone deposits, cut by hundreds of canyons and gorges, slope away toward the two ancient rivers that define the area.

MAPS

A large map titled *Canyon Country* OFF-ROAD VEHICLE TRAIL MAP - **Island Area** shows the approximate alignment of the trails described in this book, and is available from various retail outlets throughout canyon country. This map is based upon the U.S. Geological Survey 1:62,500 scale topographic quadrangles that cover the Island Area, and shows its topographic contours and features.

The southern half of the Island Area also appears on a U.S.G.S. 1:62,500 scale topographic map of Canyonlands National Park, but only the ORV trails shown within the park on this map are up to date. This map can be obtained through any U.S.G.S. retail or mail outlet, or from various visitor centers and retail outlets.

The Utah Travel Council issues a map that shows this general region, but it is of limited value for off-highway explorations.

The State Road Commission of Utah issues an official highway map that is useful for access routes to canyon country, but shows very few backcountry roads and trails.

NAVIGATION

Navigation on canyon country off-road vehicle trails is seldom simple. Several factors combine to make maps and map-reading skills essential, and even then easy trail-finding is not always assured. Some of the factors that complicate navigation are natural, but the worst are human in origin.

The principal natural factors are terrain that lacks features prominent enough to appear on topographic maps, and stretches of sand and slickrock that show few permanent traces of the trails that penetrate them.

Of the human factors, one is the lack of directional and name signs. A few of the trail and road junctions in the area covered by this book are marked by signs, but most are not.

The greatest single problem to navigation, however, is mineral search activity that obscures or realigns established trails, creates new trails, or laces huge areas with parallel and intersecting trails in support of seismographic surveys. Such operations can, within a few days, turn a huge, unspoiled natural area that was penetrated by a single obscure trail or none, into a veritable maze of bulldozed, eroding trails that destroy the natural beauty and either end at a drill site or go nowhere at all.

Since existing laws governing the search for and extraction of minerals from public land do not prevent such abusive activities, those who intend to explore canyon country by off-road vehicle must be prepared for the resulting navigational problems. The trails described in this book have all been traveled personally by the author, but as long as the mineral industry has the right to change existing trails and create new ones, there can be no assurance that any trail description will remain valid indefinitely.

Because of the noted natural and human factors, optimum trail navigation in much of canyon country consists of the skillful use of maps and the verbal descriptions in this book, plus trail-reading abilities, persistence and, in some cases, an element of luck. This is especially true in much of the area covered by this book. Only a few of the trails described are so well defined, and so protected by the surrounding terrain that they can be followed without the use of navigational skills, and most of these are within Canyonlands National Park.

BASE CAMPS

The Island Area can be explored from a variety of base camps. There are motels and commercial campgrounds within and near Moab, and developed public campgrounds at Dead Horse Point State Park and the Green River Overlook on the Island-in-the-Sky. There are also primitive campgrounds at designated sites along the White Rim Trail and its spurs. Except within the national and state parks, and on a few posted parcels of private land, primitive camping is permitted anywhere within the area covered by this book.

It should be noted that, because of the very limited access from Interstate 70 and the northernmost 15 miles of U.S. 191, the commercial facilities in the vicinity of the town of Green River do not make suitable bases for exploring most of the Island Area.

Campground, Dead Horse Point State Park

SEASONS

Because of the high-desert climate that prevails throughout the non-mountainous areas of canyon country, the best seasons for exploring the Island Area are spring, March through May, and fall, September through November. Exploration is possible during the summer, however, although daytime temperatures may occasionally exceed 100 degrees F. Most of the area can also be explored during normal winters, although even light snow may make the steeper stretches of some trails impassable.

8

ACCESS ROADS

General. Access into the Island Area from its perimeter highways, I-70, U.S. 191 and Utah 279, is by way of one paved road, Utah 313 and its extension into Canyonlands National Park, and an interconnecting system of graded dirt roads, most of them not officially named. For the purpose of this book, these have been given names by the author, names that are based upon nearby natural or manmade features. All of these interior access roads are shown on the map, *Canyon Country* OFF-ROAD VEHICLE TRAIL MAP – Island Area. The dirt roads are usually passable to two-wheel drive vehicles, but may have local bad spots or may be in generally bad condition due to recent precipitation, heavy mineral exploration traffic, lack of maintenance, or some combination of these factors.

Utah 313. This paved road leaves U.S. 191 about 8 miles north of the Colorado River bridge, penetrates scenic Sevenmile Canyon, then climbs steeply up onto the high mesa that becomes Island-in-the-Sky farther south. Here, the road crosses open sand flats studded with rounded sandstone outcroppings, with views to the north of massive redrock buttes. The road ends at Dead Horse Point, another slender extension of the same great mesa.

Island Road. This paved road branches from Utah 313 at The Knoll, about 14 miles from U.S. 191, and continues south onto the Island-in-the-Sky in Canyonlands National Park, where it branches several times to approach various overlooks and features. After this road enters the park, it offers spectacular distant views of the canyon country to the east, south and west.

Floy Wash Road. This dirt road heads south from I-70 about 13 miles east of the Green River bridge, or about 7 miles west of Crescent Junction. It travels generally southwest through relatively colorless, featureless desert until it reaches the vicinity of White Wash, where it ends at the Green River.

Blue Hills Road. This dirt road heads generally northwest from U.S. 191 just south of the airstrip of Canyonlands Field. It travels many miles of colorless, monotonous desert before connecting with the Floy Wash Road 4 miles south of I-70.

Dubinky Well Road. This dirt road travels north and south to connect the Blue Hills Road and Utah 313. It offers scenic beauty along most of its length, and passes Dubinky Well, an old windmill and stone catch-basin, along the way.

Duma Point Road. This dirt road leaves the Blue Hills Road about 13 miles from U.S. 191, then heads southwest through colorful and interesting geologic formations to become an off-road vehicle trail as it enters the Tenmile Point vicinity.

Arths Pasture Road. This dirt road leaves Utah 313 about 1-1/2 miles north of the Utah 313-Island Road junction at the Knoll to travel the ridgelands between the upper Bull and Sevenmile canyon systems and then across the broad sand flats of Arths Pasture. It provides access to several trails, including the Gemini Bridges trail, and ends as defined in this book where it joins the eastern leg of that trail.

Gold Bar Rim, right-center, viewed from Arths Rim

Circumnavigating the Merrimac, Monitor & Merrimac trail

TRAIL DESCRIPTION FORMAT

Trail name. For the purposes of this book, each trail segment described has been given a name. Where trail names are in popular use, or have appeared in print, these were used. For trails with no name history, names were assigned. Most of these were chosen from named geographic features near the trail, but in a few cases appropriate names were assigned by the author.

Trail type. As an aid to those who use this book, trail segments are classified into three types: "spur," "connecting" and "loop." A "spur" trail is a dead-end trail that has no practical connections with other trails anywhere near its end. A "connecting" trail is one that connects two or more access roads or other listed trails. A "loop" trail is one that, as described, begins and ends from the same access road or other trail, although not necessarily from the same point. A loop trail may have spurs, and may even be joined by a connecting trail, but is still a distinct stretch of trail that is worth traveling as a loop.

Maps. In this section of the trail description format, the maps most useful in navigating the trail are listed. The U.S.G.S. 1:62,500 scale topographic quadrants that cover the Island Area are not listed because their backcountry trail information is generally not up to date.

Mileage. Approximate mileages are given for each trail segment. For spur trails, the round trip distance is given. If a spur trail has other spurs, one-way mileages for these generally appear within the trail description. For connecting trails, the one-way distance is given. For loop trails, the one-way distance is given, exclusive of any spurs along the loop. One-way mileages for such spurs generally appear in the trail description.

Time. Because of the wide variety of surfaces and hazards encountered on canyon country off-road vehicle trails, plus other variables such as driving and navigational skills and time spent at stops along the way, the times to travel specific trails can only be approximated. The times given are based upon the author's experience, with all these variables taken into consideration. In each case, those who choose to "challenge the trail" will find little difficulty in bettering the times given, but in doing so will have missed most of the value of that trail.

Difficulty. Trail segments are given general ratings as to their difficulty, not for the purpose of a challenge, but to help drivers with limited experience select trails within their capabilities. Three ratings are used: "easy," "moderate" and "difficult." Such ratings are always subject to debate, because they involve personal judgment, and because no one trail is uniform for its entire length. A trail may be quite rough or difficult for most of its length, yet have easy stretches. Conversely, a trail may be predominantly two-wheel drive, yet have short stretches that are difficult even for four-wheel drive. Thus, the difficulty ratings given should be taken only in the most general sense, with exceptions to be expected along the way. In addition to trail ratings, trail surface conditions are listed under this heading. A trail may be very rough, even though rated "easy." Where there are unusually difficult or hazardous places along a trail, these are noted in the trail description.

11

Access. There is generally more than one access route to each trail segment, and the one chosen will depend upon the direction of approach. In some cases, one suggested access route is given. Those who prefer to use another route can do so by using the appropriate map, although some trails are easier to find and navigate in one direction than the other.

Trail summary. In this section, a brief summary is given of the trail's scenic highlights and other points of interest, as an aid to the selection of trails to explore.

Trail description. Each trail segment is described here at greater length than in the summary. The description covers access details, trail conditions, scenic and other highlights, spur trails where these exist, and other points of interest. In no case are such descriptions complete. Many details and highlights are left for explorers to discover for themselves, but enough are given to help those with limited time to select suitable trails, and to provide a few points to watch for along the way. With loop trails, the descriptions will begin at the loop-end that is recommended as a starting point. Explorers should consider all mileages noted in this section as approximate since odometer accuracy varies from vehicle to vehicle.

Notes. Miscellaneous information related to each trail is listed in this final section of the trail description format.

Trail's end, Sevenmile Canyon Rim trail

AREA NOTES

1. The trails in the Island Area are described as "trail segments" because most of them are interconnected in some way, making it impractical to define them otherwise. These trail segments may be explored individually, or by linking several together into routes that take half a day or more to travel. A few such routes are suggested in one section of this book.

2. National Park Service regulations require that all vehicles stay strictly on the designated off-road vehicle trails within Canyonlands National Park, and that camping be limited to designated sites. Advance reservations for these sites may be necessary.

3. The paved highways that border the Island Area are not described in this book, but are covered in another volume of the *Canyon Country* guidebook series. All three of these perimeter highways are outstandingly scenic.

4. Many of the trail segments listed have stretches that can be traveled by two-wheel drive, but all require off-road vehicles if their entire lengths are to be explored.

5. Those exploring the off-road vehicle trails in the Island Area, especially single vehicles, are advised to travel prepared for problems such as mechanical failure or getting stuck. Items that should always be carried are a spare tire, extra fuel, tools and plenty of water. An additional safety margin is afforded vehicles equipped with winches, heavy-duty roll bars and extra food in the form of freeze-dried meals.

6. Although CB radios may be of some value in calling for assistance, this value is limited during the daylight hours because of poor line-of-sight characteristics in much of the area. Night transmissions will reach farther because of atmospheric "bounce effects."

7. All historic and prehistoric sites and artifacts on public land are protected by a variety of state and federal laws. Such artifacts should not be collected, and sites should be left undisturbed.

8. Individual trail descriptions sometimes note that a trail junction "may" be marked by a sign. There are two reasons why the author could not be positive about such signs. One: vandals sometimes remove, destroy or "collect" such signs, even though such activities violate either federal or state laws. Two: of the various federal and state land administration agencies involved, only the National Park Service has an effective program for marking vehicle trail junctions with directional signs, then maintaining them. Thus, when one of the few non-Park Service signs is vandalized, it may not be replaced for years, if ever.

9. Those using this book will find that some of the trails described show very few signs of current usage. This is because such trails get very little recreational use, and only sporadic mineral-search use. Despite this, the author has explored each of the trails listed and found it to be worth sharing with those who are interested in the canyon country hinterlands.

TRAIL SEGMENTS
Alphabetical Listing

Bartlett Rim 15
Bartlett Wash 17
Bull Canyon 18
Crystal Geyser 20
Four Arches Canyon 21
Freckle Flat 24
Gemini Bridges 25
Gold Bar Rim 29
Hellroaring Canyon 31
Hidden Canyon Rim 33
Levi Well 35
Little Canyon 36
Little Canyon Rim 37
Long Canyon 39
Mineral Point 41
Monitor & Merrimac 42
Poison Spider Mesa 46
Potash 49
Rainbow Rocks 51
Red Wash 52
Salt Wash 53
Sevenmile Canyon Rim 54
Spring Canyon 57
Spring Canyon Point 61
Taylor Canyon Rim 63
Tenmile Point 65
Tenmile Wash 67
White Rim 69
White Wash 72

TRAIL DESCRIPTIONS

Trail Name: B A R T L E T T   R I M

Map: *Canyon Country* OFF-ROAD VEHICLE TRAIL MAP – Island Area

Type: Loop

Time: 2 hours; 4 hours if both spurs are explored.

Mileage: 6 miles

Difficulty: easy, with the trail surface largely sediments or packed drift sand, with a little slickrock.

Access: this loop trail leaves the Dubinky Well Road then rejoins it in the general vicinity of Dubinky Well.

Trail Summary: this loop trail and two of its spurs offer fascinating views down into colorful Bartlett Wash and its unusual tributary, Hidden Canyon.

Trail Description:

The southern end of the trail leaves the Dubinky Well Road a few yards north of a fenceline and about 4 miles north of where that road leaves Utah 313. The trail later rejoins the same road farther north. The trail first climbs slowly through rolling sand flats, but within 1-1/2 miles it rounds a rocky promontory and for the next mile closely parallels the high rim of Bartlett Wash. Along this stretch, short walks to the rim afford lovely views of the convoluted, salmon-hued sandstone bluffs that wall the broad wash on both sides.

About 2-1/2 miles from the trail start, an inconspicuous spur trail cuts sharply right. This spur is only about 1 mile long, but offers fascinating views down into Bartlett Wash and its tributary, maze-like Hidden Canyon, from where the trail ends on a high promontory.

About 3/4 mile beyond this junction, a second spur heads right onto a rocky point, then descends a steep hill of reddish sediments to the level of the northern rim of Hidden Canyon, where it joins the Hidden Canyon Rim Trail.

A third spur trail angles gently to the right from the main loop trail about 1-1/2 miles beyond the first spur junction. This spur is rough, offers still other views of Hidden Canyon within a few yards of the trail, and becomes rather challenging for the last mile or so before it ends on a rocky point, 2-1/2 miles from where it begins.

From the third spur junction, the main loop trail continues for about 2-1/2 miles through interesting sandflats and slickrock country before ending at the Dubinky Well Road 1-1/4 miles north of the Dubinky Well windmill, and about 4 miles north of where the loop started.

Note: Another trail segment described later in this book reaches the northern rim of Hidden Canyon, while a spur to the Bartlett Wash trail sometimes permits entry into the canyon.

Bartlett Rim

"The Submarine," in Bartlett Wash, aerial view

Trail Name: B A R T L E T T   W A S H

Map: *Canyon Country* OFF-ROAD VEHICLE TRAIL MAP - **Island Area**

Type: Connecting

Time: 1 hour; 3 hours or more if Hidden Canyon is explored.

Mileage: 7-1/2 miles

Difficulty: easy, with most of the trail surface wash or drift sand, plus some slickrock in the upper wash.

Access: this trail connects the Dubinky Well Road with either the Blue Hills Road or Monitor & Merrimac trail.

Trail Summary: this connecting trail travels the length of colorful Bartlett Wash, closely paralleling one of its picturesque sandstone walls most of the way.

Trail Description:

The trail leaves the Monitor & Merrimac trail where that trail climbs out of lower Tusher Canyon, then immediately climbs a steep sand hill. For the next mile, the trail wanders among low, rocky hills before joining a spur from the Blue Hills Road (see Note 2.). It then turns left into lower Bartlett Wash. The trail next goes through the close-walled narrows of the lower wash, before climbing onto higher ground.

In this vicinity, an inconspicuous spur trail leaves the main trail to the right, drops steeply into a side-wash, then follows this deep, twisting wash through a narrow gap in the reddish sandstone cliffs that wall the main wash, to enter Hidden Canyon. The sandy, branching wash bottoms within this mazelike side-canyon can be negotiated for short distances, but hiking offers the best views of this fascinating place.

The main trail continues up Bartlett Wash beyond this spur junction, closely following the looming northern wall. Other spurs branch left off of this trail. One of these approaches and parallels the southern wall of the wash and eventually reaches the Dubinky Well Road. The main trail climbs steadily, enters an expanse of rough slickrock, then connects with the Dubinky Well Road about 3 miles north of its junction with Utah 313, and 3/4 mile south of one end of the Bartlett Rim loop trail.

Notes:

1. The up-canyon direction through Bartlett Wash is described here because this makes a good combination route with the Monitor & Merrimac trail, as detailed in a later section of this book.

2. To reach Bartlett Wash from the Blue Hills Road, watch for an unmarked trail heading south from that road about 2-1/2 miles west of U.S. 191. Turn left onto this trail, left again in about 3/4 mile, right in another 3/4 mile, then continue southward into Bartlett Wash.

3. Flash flooding can cause minor trail realignments in the narrows of Bartlett Wash, and may leave the spur trail into Hidden Canyon impassable to vehicles.

Trail Name: B U L L   C A N Y O N

Map: *Canyon Country* OFF-ROAD VEHICLE TRAIL MAP - **Island Area**

Type: Spur

Time: 3 hours; 5 hours if the two spurs are explored.

Mileage: 7 miles round trip

Difficulty: easy, with the trail surface largely slickrock, wash sand, drift sand and packed sediments.

Access: this trail segment is a major spur from the Gemini Bridges trail, or from the Gold Bar Rim trail by way of the Little Canyon connecting trail.

Trail Summary: this spur trail provides access to the canyon below the Gemini Bridges and, together with one long and one short spur trail, provides a close look at the lower ends of the two main branches of Bull Canyon and their spectacular junction with Day Canyon.

Trail Description:

The Bull Canyon trail branches south from the Gemini Bridges trail about 5-1/2 miles after that trail leaves U.S. 191, or about 8-1/2 miles from Utah 313. It then travels through rough sand and slickrock terrain, meets the Little Canyon connecting trail after about 1-1/2 miles, then drops down into the lower wash of Bull Canyon, where its two main branches join. A 1/4-mile spur trail down this wash ends at a breathtaking dry waterfall hundreds of feet high, with two unusual natural bridges and a water-carved, slickrock grotto at the brink of the drop.

At the Bull Canyon fork, the left spur penetrates the Dry Fork of Bull Canyon for about 2-1/2 miles before the trail becomes impassable due to erosion. Near the end of this canyon-bottom spur, there are several old mines, a dry reservoir and a partly exposed petrified forest.

The main Bull Canyon trail goes up the right fork from the trail junction in the wash. Because of tilted strata, the trail begins in a shallow wash, but as it continues, the canyon walls grow to spectacular heights, exhibiting beautiful contours and erosional forms. About 2 miles up this canyon, a trail spur to the right enters a 1/2-mile long, box-end side-canyon. The spectacular Gemini Bridges span the upper end of this short canyon, but are visible only from near its upper end.

The main trail continues up Bull Canyon for about 2 more miles, becoming impassable because of erosion in the vicinity of some old mines. There are several inconspicuous arches in the cliffs of this Bull Canyon branch, and traces of the petrified forest exposed in the parallel canyon can also be found here.

Notes:

1. It is not legal to collect more than small specimens of petrified wood on public land.

2. Entering old mine shafts can be very hazardous.

3. Trail stretches in or near canyon wash bottoms are subject to severe damage from flash flooding.

Gemini Bridges, Bull Canyon trail

Trail Name: C R Y S T A L   G E Y S E R

Map: *Canyon Country* OFF-ROAD VEHICLE TRAIL MAP - Island Area

Type: Connecting

Time: 3 hours; 3-1/2 hours if the Crystal Geyser spur is taken.

Mileage: 14-1/2 miles

Difficulty: easy, with the trail largely packed sediments or drift sand, with some wash sand and slickrock.

Access: this trail connects Interstate 70 and the Salt Wash trail.

Trail Summary: this trail provides a look at a cold-water geyser, stretches of the Green River above Labyrinth Canyon, and colorful, broken expanses of painted desert, with good rock collecting along the way.

Trail Description:

The trail turns south about 4 miles east of the Green River, or about 15 miles west of Crescent Junction. After the first 1/2 mile or so, the road enters picturesque, colorful painted desert country studded with protruding rock formations.

About 5 miles from the trail start, the trail forks. The right fork is a 1/2-mile spur that goes to Crystal Geyser, beside the Green River. At intervals, this cold-water geyser erupts with a fountain of highly mineralized water. These minerals form beautiful terraces of brownish crystals on the slopes between the geyser and the river.

The left fork of the trail continues generally south, closely paralleling the river for about 2 miles. It then passes near private ranchlands in a broad riverbottom. About 7-1/2 miles from I-70, the trail reaches a confusing trail junction in the vicinity of a shallow, sandy drywash. The main trail continues southward, roughly parallel to the river, then climbs onto higher ground to round a low butte within sight of the river. It then leaves the river to go up a broad, shallow painted desert valley. About 3 miles beyond the drywash junction, the trail briefly travels a ridge that overlooks an exceptionally colorful expanse of painted desert formations, then drops down to continue up another small desert valley.

About 4-1/4 miles from the drywash junction, the trail forks. The main trail goes left here, climbs more steeply for 1/2 mile to another trail fork, where it turns right to descend steeply into still another desert valley. It crosses this valley, climbs onto an expanse of eroded slickrock, then drops into a series of shallow gullies and canyons. In one of these, the trail ends by joining the Salt Wash trail, about 1 mile from where that trail ends overlooking the Green River.

Notes:

1. The main attractions along this trail are Crystal Geyser, colorful painted desert landscapes, close views of the Green River above Labyrinth Canyon and good rockhounding.

2. This trail is not recommended during the warmer months of July and August.

3. The privately owned structures seen several places along this trail should not be disturbed in any way.

4. There are several spurs to this trail worth exploring if time permits, but most such spurs are mineral exploration trails that go nowhere.

Pioneer cabin, near Crystal Geyser trail

Trail Name: F O U R   A R C H E S   C A N Y O N

Map: *Canyon Country* OFF-ROAD VEHICLE TRAIL MAP – **Island Area**

Type: Spur

Time: 2 hours; 3 hours if the one spur is explored.

Mileage: 4 miles round trip

Difficulty: easy, with the trail surface largely packed drift sand or sediments, and some wash-bottom sand.

Access: this trail segment is a spur of the Gemini Bridges trail.

Trail Summary: this spur trail enters the colorful and lovely upper reaches of Bull Canyon, where in one short stretch of trail four large and beautiful arches are visible in the canyon walls.

21

Trail Description:

This trail heads south from the Gemini Bridges trail about 3/4 mile east of where that trail leaves the Arths Pasture Road, and about 1 mile west of the trail spur that goes to the tops of the Gemini Bridges. The trail immediately drops down into Crips Hole, a grassy valley in upper Bull Canyon, then forks in the wash bottom. The left spur is about 1-1/4 miles long and ends in a narrow, lovely branch of the canyon system.

The right fork is the main trail. It crosses a short stretch of wash-bottom slickrock, then climbs onto the open sand flats that lie between the canyon walls here, but soon enters the narrow upper canyon, following the power lines that serve Dead Horse Point State Park. These are the only unsightly characteristic in an otherwise lovely, high-walled canyon.

Soon after the canyon narrows, two arches on the right wall can be seen. One is a large, slender jughandle-type, with only a narrow slit behind it. Its name is Bullwhip Arch. From one angle it can be seen that this opening is actually double.

The other arch in the right wall is high above the canyon floor and shaped somewhat like a huge elephant's trunk, or a mosquito's proboscis. Its name is Mosquito Arch.

The second two arches are high in the left wall of the canyon and shortly beyond the others. Both are large, arch-shaped openings in huge sandstone fins that jut from the cliff at right angles. Both are also obscured by other wall outcroppings and are hence difficult to locate. The first arch is called Shadow Arch. The less obvious second one is Crips Arch.

Beyond these four arches, the trail continues for about 1 mile, to end at the point where the power lines swing sharply up to poles on the high canyon rim. One steep grade about 1/4 mile from the trail end may be impassable due to erosion and loose surface rock.

Notes:

1. The wash bottom stretches of this trail are subject to damage from flash flooding.

2. With care, it is possible to free-climb up to the two arches in the right wall of the canyon, and almost to the first arch in the left wall. Climbing aids and skills are necessary in order to actually reach either of the left wall spans.

3. An obscure spur trail from Utah 313 can be followed to reach the point on the rim where the power lines leave the canyon, but a gigantic cleft bars access to the cliff above the two arches farther along the same canyon rim. Another obscure and unmapped trail that leaves Utah 313 in the vicinity of The Knoll leads to within a short hike of the canyon rim opposite Shadow Arch.

4. The first public record of the four major arches near the end of this trail was an article by this author, who found and photographed all four of the spans in the winter of 1974-75, then published the photos in an article titled "Four Arches" in a travel guide titled "Canyon Country Trails & Highlights #3," dated August 1975.

5. The main wash into which this trail first descends makes an interesting hike as it penetrates one long branch of the upper Bull Canyon system. Just beyond where the canyon first narrows, there is a double arch high on the left wall.

Mosquito Arch, Four Arches trail

Shadow Arch, Four Arches trail

Trail Name: F R E C K L E   F L A T

Map: *Canyon Country* OFF-ROAD VEHICLE TRAIL MAP - **Island Area**

Type: Connecting

Time: 1/2 hour or less

Mileage: 4-1/2 miles

Difficulty: easy, with the trail surface largely slickrock and loose or packed drift sand.

Access: this trail connects the Spring Canyon Point trail with the Tenmile Wash, Levi Well and Rainbow Rocks trails.

Trail Summary: this trail crosses rolling, open sand and slickrock terrain and is listed because it provides a useful connection between four other trail segments and offers excellent panoramic views of the nearby redrock buttes and colorful desert that surrounds them.

Trail Description:

The trail branches from the Spring Canyon Point trail about 1-1/2 miles west of a point called "The Needles." It then heads north, offering distant views of several large redrock buttes and mesas to the east before ending at the Levi Well-Tenmile Wash trail junction 1/2 mile west of a wash-bottom spring and several isolated cottonwood trees. There is good rockhounding at several points along the trail.

Note:

Mineral exploration activities in this vicinity have left a network of trails that can confuse navigation even along this short connecting trail.

Trail Name: G E M I N I   B R I D G E S

Type: Connecting

Map: *Canyon Country* OFF-ROAD VEHICLE TRAIL MAP - Island Area

Mileage: 10 miles

Time: 3 hours; 6 hours or more if the Bull Canyon spur trail to below the Gemini Bridges is explored.

Difficulty: easy, with the trail surface largely packed sediments and drift sand, rubble, slickrock and wash sand.

Access: this trail connects U.S. 191 and Utah 313 via Arths Pasture Road.

Trail Summary: this trail enters the spectacularly distorted sandstone wilderness region that lies to the west of the cliffs that loom above U.S. 191 north of the Colorado River, and provides access to the breathtaking and unique Gemini Bridges and several other outstanding trail segments.

View from near Gemini Bridges

25

Trail Description:

This long and interesting trail branches from U.S. 191 about 7 miles north of the Colorado River Bridge, and 1-1/2 miles south of the U.S. 191-Utah 313 junction. It goes through a cattle control fence, heads left on top of an embankment that protects a railroad cut from water runoff, then turns right to cross rolling red sandflats country before climbing abruptly up the tilted, colorful strata at the base of the high cliffs to the west of U.S. 191. Next, the trail enters Little Canyon, which can be seen from below as a large gap in the western cliff line. Rock collectors will find the first mile or so of this strange "hanging canyon" rewarding.

About 1-1/2 miles into the canyon, a short spur left enters a box-end canyon. The Bride, a colorful and slender sandstone spire, and two arches are in the left wall of this canyon. The first, Owl Arch, is two caves high in the cliff that have joined. The other span is small and not easy to locate, but can be seen on the left skyline from one short stretch of the trail.

The main trail next passes the base of a towering rock spire called "The Gooney Bird," or "de Gaulle Stone," then crosses a broad, sandy wash. The trail down this wash is the Gold Bar Rim trail. A short trail spur just beyond the wash goes right to a curious arch in the low canyon wall.

The Gemini Bridges trail climbs a steep slope of fill material, then continues to ascend terraced slickrock slopes for another mile before leveling off in broken sand and slickrock terrain. Here, it passes junctions with the Little Canyon Rim and Bull Canyon trails.

About 1/2 mile beyond the junction with the Bull Canyon trail, the Gemini Bridges trail angles left from what seems to be the main trail, just before a series of ascending curves. The graded dirt road that continues right here is the Arths Pasture Road, which the Gemini Bridges trail rejoins at its west end. Beyond this junction, which may have a sign, the Gemini Bridges trail is sometimes more difficult to find and follow.

About 2-1/2 miles from where the trail climbs out of Little Canyon, it enters the broad, open sandflats country of Arths Pasture and almost immediately a short spur trail goes left down a series of slickrock terraces toward the Gemini Bridges. This spur is moderately difficult and confused by false trails.

For those who prefer, it is easy to walk the 1/4 mile between the main trail and the bridges, which were named after the legendary Gemini Twins. The trail spur to the spans actually loops across one of them, but driving across can be hazardous.

Near the bridges, still another short trail spur goes south a few yards to reach the canyon rim at a spectacular point, where the panoramic view is outstanding. About 1 mile beyond the bridges spur trail junction, the main trail passes the Four Arches spur trail and then rejoins Arths Pasture Road just east of where the Sevenmile Canyon Rim trail branches from that road.

Utah 313 is about 4 miles west of the Gemini Bridges-Arths Pasture Road junction.

Notes:

1. There may be signs on this trail at its junctions with U.S. 191 and Arths Pasture Road, on that road's junction with Utah 313, at the trail spur to the tops of the bridges, and at the Four Arches and Bull Canyon trail junctions.

2. The natural bridges reached by this trail were officially
named "Gemini Bridges" by the Department of the Interior Board on
Geographic Names in 1969, on Decision List 6901.

3. Those who have limited time, but want to see the Gemini
Bridges, can take this trail from Utah 313 and Arths Pasture Road
to the bridge spur, then return the same way. When going to the
bridges from this direction, turn right onto the Gemini Bridges
trail about 4 miles from Utah 313, then left at the Four Arches
trail junction in about another 1/2 mile. The spur right to the
Gemini Bridges is about 1 mile beyond this second trail fork.

Gemini Bridges, Gemini Bridges trail

Gold Bar Rim

Trail Name: G O L D   B A R   R I M

Map: *Canyon Country* OFF-ROAD VEHICLE TRAIL MAP - **Island Area**

Type: Spur

Time: 3 hours; longer if the spur trails are explored.

Mileage: 7-1/2 miles round trip; more if either of the two branching spurs are explored.

Difficulty: moderate with short difficult stretches, with the trail surface partly wash sand and packed drift sand, but largely rough, steep slickrock.

Access: this trail is a major spur to the Gemini Bridges trail.

Trail Summary: this spur trail climbs the immense sandstone slope that lies beyond the cliffs to the west of U.S. 191 north of the Colorado River bridge, and ends at a high rim point that offers a breathtaking, full-circle view. A rough spur connects it to another trail, making the two a loop trail.

Trail Description:

The trail leaves the Gemini Bridges trail in the wash bottom of Little Canyon, about 5 miles from U.S. 191. It goes down the wash for about 1/2 mile, then climbs steeply out to the left.

For the next 1/2 mile or so the trail climbs through broken, rocky terrain with occasional wash sand or packed drift sand. At a trail junction in a small meadow area about 1 mile from the trail start and about 1/2 mile from where it leaves Little Canyon wash, the Little Canyon connecting trail forks right.

The main trail goes left at this junction, to reach a second fork in another 1/2 mile. The spur right here ends in 1 mile, but offers a 1/2 mile hiking access to spectacular Jeep Arch.

The main trail goes left at this junction. In about 3/4 mile another obscure trail spurs left to travel along a ledge, as the main trail is descending to cross a shallow drainage line. This spur travels generally northwestward to reach the canyon rim overlooking The Bride, a tall spire reached from the Gemini Bridges trail, travels the canyon rim, then descends slickrock to the rim of Little Canyon, near the Gooney Bird spire.

Beyond this spur junction, the main trail crosses a wash, climbs again, descends to cross upper Gold Bar Canyon, then climbs steeply along the slender ridge of sandstone that separates that deep gorge and another one. About 1 mile beyond the spur to The Bride overlook, the main trail reaches Lunch Rock, an undercut, flat-topped rock mass perched on the spectacular rim of Gold Bar Canyon that offers a shady and highly scenic setting for lunch.

Just beyond Lunch Rock, the trail angles down to the left, then climbs steeply on sandstone slickrock for about 1/2 mile to a final junction just below Gold Bar Rim. The left spur climbs several rocky ledges, then ends directly on the rim. Since turning around here is awkward and hazardous, it is advisable that only one or two vehicles actually go all the way, with any others parking below the last ledges.

The right spur also climbs several steep ledges, to end on a broad sandstone slope that offers ample parking and spectacular views in all directions.

The Gold Bar Rim panorama overlooks the gorge through which U.S. 191 climbs out of Moab Valley, with Arches National Park beyond to the east. To the southeast, Moab Valley stretches out toward the distant La Sal Mountains, and Gold Bar Rim extends in the same direction to become a part of Poison Spider Mesa.

To the south and southwest, the meandering Colorado River gorge and some of its tributary canyons can be seen beyond the immense sandstone slope that the trail has climbed. Toward the northwest, the high rim and slickrock slope continue until cut by Little Canyon, becoming Arths Pasture Rim beyond that canyon.

Notes:

1. If the trail is lost on a stretch of slickrock, one approach is to have someone walk ahead searching for traces of wheel tracks and the place where the trail leaves the rock. This prevents navigational errors and the creation of misleading tracks.

2. Whatever technique is used to find this trail on the way up to the rim, it is well to note landmarks to use for guidance on the way back down.

3. By hiking to the right along Gold Bar Rim from the trail end, Jeep Arch can be seen in a huge redrock outcropping about 2 miles to the southeast. Binoculars will aid such viewing.

Colorado River gorge, from Gold Bar Rim

Trail Name: H E L L R O A R I N G   C A N Y O N

Map: *Canyon Country* OFF-ROAD VEHICLE TRAIL MAP - Island Area

Type: Spur

Mileage: 18 miles round trip

Time: 3 hours; 4 hours if the Mineral Canyon spur is explored.

Difficulty: easy for several miles up the canyon, with the trail surface either packed sediments or wash-bottom sand and rock; difficult on up the canyon, if passable at all.

Access: this trail is a major spur to the White Rim Trail, but is outside of Canyonlands National Park.

Trail Summary: this trail goes up the spectacular Green River gorge, then penetrates for several miles up one of that gorge's major tributaries, Hellroaring Canyon.

Trail Description:

The Hellroaring Canyon trail branches from the White Rim trail at the base of the Mineral Canyon switchbacks that descend to the Green River. The trail junction is about 15 miles from Utah 313. From this junction, the trail goes upriver below the high cliffs and talus slopes of the gorge and closely parallel to the river.

About 1-1/2 miles from the trail junction, a spur trail goes up Mineral Canyon for about 5-1/2 miles to a major canyon fork, then continues up the right fork. Mineral Canyon is deep and narrow, with active and inactive uranium mines at intervals. This spur trail may be impassable due to erosion and lack of maintenance.

On the main trail up the rivergorge, the remains of a uranium mining community can be seen below the cliffs about 2 miles from the trail start. In another 2 miles, the trail turns up Hellroaring Canyon. Within this spectacular canyon, the trail travels within or near the wash bottom, but becomes virtually impassable beyond about 5 miles into the canyon, where boulders block the trail, and it is not possible to bypass the blockage.

Notes:

1. All of the slopes above the trail beside the river and in Hellroaring Canyon offer good rock collecting.

2. Beyond the boulder-blocked part of the canyon, the old trail continues for about 2 miles. Exploring the rest of this long canyon and its tributaries must be on foot. The trail up Hellroaring may not be passable for all of the first 5 miles.

3. There is a developed dirt boat-launch ramp into the Green River at a point 1 mile from the beginning of this trail. This ramp is commonly used by boaters for both access and egress.

4. There is a large natural arch in the extreme upper end of Hellroaring Canyon. A trail spur from Utah 313 skirts around the canyon rim above this arch.

Hellroaring Canyon

Trail Name: H I D D E N   C A N Y O N   R I M

Map: *Canyon Country* OFF-ROAD VEHICLE TRAIL MAP - **Island Area**

Type: Spur

Time: 3 hours; 3-1/2 hours if a short side trail is explored.

Mileage: 8 miles round trip

Difficulty: easy, with the trail surface largely packed sediments, drift sand and slickrock.

Access: this trail heads southward from the Blue Hills Road several miles west of U.S. 191.

Trail Summary: this short but very interesting trail provides rim views down into two lovely hidden canyons and an unusual slickrock valley.

Hidden Canyon Rim

Trail Description:

This trail angles sharply left off of the Blue Hills road about 3-1/2 miles west of U.S. 191. Although the first part of this trail is shown on The Knoll topographic quadrangle, its junction has been confused by more recent mineral exploration trails. After 1/2 mile across barren desert, the trail crosses a shallow, wooded wash, then within another 1/2 mile angles right into a canyon, where it soon reaches Brink Spring.

There, a perennial spring has been developed for use by cattle, and the picturesque remains of an old cabin stand on a low hill above the watering troughs. The trail climbs steeply past and above this cabin, then crosses a slickrock flat before reaching and paralleling the rim of deep, narrow and lovely Brink Spring Canyon, that run-off has carved out of solid sandstone.

After another mile, most of it on slickrock that makes navigation difficult, the trail reaches an inconspicuous trail junction. The right fork climbs steeply over a low ridge to enter an unusual slickrock expanse called Lunar Canyon, from its resemblance to the bright, arid surface of the moon.

The main trail continues in a southwestward direction and in about 1 mile angles sharply left to drop down into a rolling, wooded expanse of drift sand. Here, the route is confused by several old mineral search trails, but goes in a generally eastward direction to reach the terraced rim of Hidden Canyon after about 1/2 mile.

An old, eroded mineral search trail continues to the right in this vicinity, but soon ends at another overlook on the same canyon rim. Another spur parallels the rim farther back, to ascend a very steep slope of reddish sediments, then travel a rocky promontory before joining the Bartlett Rim trail.

Notes:

1. It is possible to explore Brink Spring Canyon by hiking down from where the vehicle trail first reaches its rim. The drainage line above the pour-off into this canyon is also worth hiking.

2. Do not to disturb the old cabin at Brink Spring.

Brinks Spring Canyon

Trail Name: L E V I   W E L L

Map: *Canyon Country* OFF-ROAD VEHICLE TRAIL MAP - Island Area

Type: Connecting

Mileage: 7 miles

Time: 1 hour

Difficulty: easy, with the trail surface largely packed sediments, packed or loose drift sand and a few rocky places.

Access: this trail connects the Blue Hills Road with the Tenmile Wash, Freckle Flat and Rainbow Rocks trails.

Trail Summary: this trail penetrates low, hilly desertlands, then travels for several miles between the picturesque redrock walls of Tenmile Wash, passing a curious desert spring along the way.

Trail Description:

The trail leaves the Blue Hills Road less than 1/4 mile west of that road's junction with the Dubinky Well Road. It then winds through relatively colorless desert hills that may be of interest to rock collectors and, after about 2 miles, reaches Levi Well. Here, beside a fenceline, spring water flows out of a pipe and out across the desert, creating a marshy, verdant oasis.

The trail goes through a gate in this fence, then continues westward. Just beyond this gate, a spur trail to the left climbs into the rocky terrain to the south, but the main trail continues generally westward for about 2 miles before entering broad Tenmile Wash to travel through drift sand country near one picturesque slickrock wall. A line of cottonwood trees in the nearby wash tells of perennial subsurface moisture there.

As the slickrock wall curves away from the wash, the Rainbow Rocks trail joins the Levi Well trail just a few yards east of a seeping, wash-bottom spring where several isolated cottonwoods grow. The Levi Well trail joins the Freckle Flat and Tenmile Wash trails about 1/2 mile beyond this wash.

Note: The slickrock butte that walls Tenmile Wash on the south is one end of the twisting, 15-mile long Rainbow Rocks butte.

Trail Name: L I T T L E   C A N Y O N

Map: *Canyon Country* OFF-ROAD VEHICLE TRAIL MAP – **Island Area**

Type: Connecting

Time: 1 hour

Mileage: 3 miles

Difficulty: easy, with the trail surface largely packed sediments or drift sand, with some slickrock and loose rubble.

Access: this trail connects the Gold Bar Rim and Bull Canyon trails.

Trail Summary: this trail provides a convenient connection between the Gold Bar Rim and Bull Canyon trails, but is well worth traveling for the scenic beauty it offers as it winds through the very broken sandstone terrain that surrounds the middle reaches of Little Canyon.

Trail Description:

      This scenic connecting trail leaves the Gold Bar Rim trail about 1/2 mile from where that trail first climbs out of the Little Canyon wash bottom. It first goes in a southward direction for about 1/2 mile before dropping back down to cross the Little Canyon wash.
      It then climbs steeply up rocky terraces and slopes toward a sandstone promontory that looks like a gigantic tortoise, then around it to the right to top out on a high, flat ridge which offers excellent panoramic views of the surrounding sandstone wilderness.
      A short distance to the west of this ridge, the descending trail joins the Bull Canyon trail, about 1-1/2 miles from the Bull Canyon-Gemini Bridges trail junction.

Notes:

1. The hike down the wash bottom from where this trail crosses Little Canyon is highly rewarding.

2. This trail is confused by several mineral search trails in the vicinity of the high, flat ridge it crosses.

Trail Name: L I T T L E   C A N Y O N   R I M

Map: *Canyon Country* OFF-ROAD VEHICLE TRAIL MAP - **Island Area**

Type: Spur

Time: 3 hours

Mileage: 12 miles round trip, slightly shorter if the optional approach trail is used.

Difficulty: moderate, with the trail surface largely rough or broken slickrock and some packed drift sand.

Access: this trail is a spur from the Arths Pasture Road, and can also be reached from the Sevenmile Canyon Rim trail by way of a 1-mile connecting spur.

Trail Summary: this spectacular and challenging trail provides access to the upper end of a deep and lovely arm of Little Canyon and offers views down into the beautiful main branch of that canyon from a lofty and breathtaking slickrock rim.

Little Canyon, from Little Canyon Rim

Trail Description:

There are two approaches to this trail. One leaves the Gemini Bridges trail about 3/4 mile after that trail leaves the Little Canyon wash to climb into higher terrain. The trail is rough, not always easy to find, and somewhat confused by mineral search trails. It appears to end about 2-1/2 miles from the Gemini Bridges trail on an expanse of slickrock, but joins the other approach just north of there.

The second and recommended approach begins from the Arths Pasture Road, about 2 miles from the Little Canyon wash, or about 3/4 mile beyond where the Gemini Bridges trail forks left and the Arths Pasture Road begins.

From this junction, the Little Canyon Rim trail goes right for about 1/2 mile then right again toward the northeast. In about 1/3 mile, the trail goes near the white sandstone expanse that marks the other approach, then in another 3/4 mile drops into and crosses a sandy wash. The 1/2-mile hike down this wash to where it plunges abruptly into a narrow arm of Little Canyon is quite interesting all the way.

From the wash, the vehicle trail climbs steeply toward the broad, tilted expanse of slickrock to the east. Along the next 2 miles of trail, it is intersected by several old mineral-search trails, but most of these show little use, making the main trail fairly easy to follow except where it crosses a large expanse of bare sandstone.

About 2 miles beyond the wash, the trail reaches and closely parallels the lofty rim of Little Canyon, offering spectacular views of the canyon and the La Sal Mountains in the distance.

The recommended trail ends in another 1/2 mile, just beyond where it skirts around the head of a plunging canyon system. A connecting spur trail continues beyond this point, to join the Sevenmile Canyon Rim trail near its end. This spur is virtually impassable going from the end of the Little Canyon Rim trail, but hiking its 1/2-mile length leads to Arths Rim. The panoramic views from this lofty rim make the hike well worthwhile.

Notes:

1. It is well to note landmarks along this trail on the way up to the rim, to use for guidance on the way back down.

2. The same techniques used for trail-finding across the slickrock on the Gold Bar Rim trail will be useful on this trail.

3. The short but extremely steep and rough ORV spur trail that connects the end of this trail to Arths Rim and the end of the Sevenmile Canyon Rim trail can be taken in the down direction from the rim, in order to make the two trails a loop.

38

Trail Name: L O N G C A N Y O N

Map: *Canyon Country* OFF-ROAD VEHICLE TRAIL MAP - **Island Area**

Type: Connecting

Time: 3/4 hour; 1 hour if a short spur is explored.

Mileage: 7 miles

Difficulty: easy, with the trail surface largely graded dirt, with a few steep, rough and rocky stretches near the top of the grade.

Access: this trail connects Utah 279 and Utah 313.

Trail Summary: this highly scenic trail climbs from the Colorado River gorge via a deep, narrow and colorful canyon, up onto the great elevated mesa that becomes the Island-in-the-Sky at its southern end, with breathtaking views back into and beyond the rivergorge most of the way.

Long Canyon

39

Trail Description:

This spectacular trail leaves Utah 279 immediately downriver of Jughandle Arch and about 2 miles before the pavement ends at the potash plant. The trail enters deep and narrow Long Canyon, then begins to climb a grade that gets continually steeper until it tops out at the head of the canyon. There are many switchback curves and enchanting views back down the canyon along the way, especially in the upper half of the canyon.

After a final rough, steep grade, the trail levels off where a huge, slender peninsula of rock forms a gigantic "Y" out of the upper end of the canyon. Here, a short spur trail goes out onto the peninsula. A walk beyond the spur end provides breathtaking views toward the Colorado River gorge and the fantastic slickrock fin country beyond that is called "Behind the Rocks."

From this spur trail, the main trail gradually climbs still higher onto the mesaland to join paved Utah 313 about 3 miles after leaving Long Canyon.

Notes:

1. Toward the end of the jutting peninsula that splits upper Long Canyon, it is possible to see down through a narrow crevice in the slickrock to the canyon floor hundreds of feet below.

2. There are other spur trails that go to the north from this trail on the mesa top. One of these can be used to reach the canyon rim above the Four Arches trail where the power lines leave the canyon. Others travel the elevated peninsulas that divide other branches of the Bull and Day canyon systems.

End of spur, Long Canyon trail

40

Trail Name: M I N E R A L   P O I N T

Map: *Canyon Country* OFF-ROAD VEHICLE TRAIL MAP - Island Area

Time: 4 hours

Type: Spur

Mileage: 27 miles round trip

Difficulty: easy, with the trail surface largely packed sediments or drift sand, and a little slickrock.

Access: this trail spurs west off of Utah 313 about 3 miles south of the Utah 313-Dubinky Well junction, about 3 miles north of the Utah 313-Island Road junction at The Knoll, and a few yards north of the Utah 313-White Rim trail junction.

Trail Summary: this trail provides access to a spectacular point overlooking the Green River gorge.

Trail Description:

The trail travels relatively flat, open sandflats country set with low domes and ridges of slickrock for its entire length. Numerous old mineral search trails confuse navigation and detract from the scenic beauty along some of the trail.

After about 7 miles, a trail fork to the right goes around a ridge to enter a small, hidden valley. This spur ends at the site of an old stock pond after about 1-1/2 miles.

The main trail continues in a southwestward direction for another 5-1/2 miles before reaching the rim of the spectacular Green River gorge. The main trail ends at a point on the rim where the mouth of Hellroaring Canyon can be seen just upriver.

A short spur trail to the left, plus a short walk, leads to another breathtaking overlook. There, it is possible to see the mouth of Mineral Canyon, an abandoned uranium mining area directly below, the lower end of the White Rim trail switchbacks that descend to the river level, the boat launch ramp noted in the Hellroaring Canyon trail description, and several sweeping bends in the rivergorge.

Notes:

1. Although this trail is not worthwhile in itself, and goes through terrain scarred by past mineral search activities, the viewpoints it reaches make this trail worth taking.

2. This trail has numerous spurs. Most are mineral search trails that go nowhere, but a few continue into other interesting mesa-top areas worth exploring if time is available.

41

Trail Name: M O N I T O R & M E R R I M A C

Map: *Canyon Country* OFF-ROAD VEHICLE TRAIL MAP - **Island Area**

Time: 6 hours; 7 hours if the two spurs are explored.

Type: Loop

Mileage: about 17 miles for the basic trail

Difficulty: easy, with trail surfaces largely packed or loose drift sand, rough slickrock, wash sand or packed sediments, with wet sand and water possible in two stretches.

Access: this loop trail begins and ends at U.S. 191, but also connects with the Bartlett Wash trail and Utah 313.

Trail Summary: this trail offers a wide variety of scenic beauty, including panoramic viewpoints, natural spans, gigantic redrock buttes, mesas and spires, rock collecting, stream-watered canyons and two challenging stretches of trail.

Merrimac Butte, Monitor & Merrimac trail

Trail Description:

This interesting and varied trail heads west from U.S. 191 about 12-1/2 miles north of the Colorado River bridge, or 4-1/4 miles north of the U.S. 191-Utah 313 junction. It crosses the railroad tracks, then goes through open washes and desert for about 1/2 mile before reaching a trail junction. The right fork is the other end of this loop trail.

The route described goes left here and in about 1/2 mile crosses a shallow wash that is sometimes wet. A spur trail to the right here goes to the partly-restored remains of an historic wagon-route station visible west of the main trail.

Beyond the shallow wash, the trail climbs gradually in a southerly direction, going to the east of the huge butte called Courthouse Rock. At a trail fork about 2 miles from the trail start, the left fork descends to a mining area at the base of the cliffs, then goes on to U.S. 191, but the main trail turns right to climb steeply toward the slickrock terraces at the base of Courthouse Rock. About 1/2 mile beyond this junction, the trail passes the site of an annual sand-hill-climbing competition.

The trail continues south on slickrock, climbing into the still higher sand and slickrock country of Courthouse Pasture, to reach a broad, level area of white slickrock to the right of the trail that offers a panoramic view of the entire area.

About 1/2 mile beyond this viewpoint, and 3-1/2 miles from the trail start, the trail forks again, almost due west of the head of Corral Canyon, which is a sharply cut gorge visible to the east. Here, the left fork is the described route. The optional trail straight ahead goes directly toward the distant Monitor & Merrimac buttes across open sand flats and can be taken by those with limited time.

The trail to the left descends to cross a small wash in about 1/2 mile. Mineral search trails in this area confuse navigation beyond this point, but the main trail goes in a generally eastward direction toward the high rim visible to the south of Corral Canyon, climbing steeply and reaching the rim about 3/4 mile beyond the wash. The rim offers spectacular panoramic views in all directions. Note odometer mileage when the rim is first reached.

About 1/2 mile along the rim, a few hundred feet south of a huge slickrock promontory that juts out from the rim, a 1/4-mile hike down a shallow drainage line in the western slickrock slope goes to a large natural bridge named "Uranium Arch."

The trail continues closely parallel to the eastern rim for about another 1/2 mile, then leaves it at the base of the rocky promontory that marks one rim of upper Sevenmile Canyon. The panoramic view from the top of this sandstone hill is excellent. Beyond here, the trail is marked by occasional small rock cairns.

About 1/3 mile after leaving the eastern rim, the trail angles left and climbs a sandstone ridge. In another 1/4 mile, it angles left again, down through a stretch of reddish sediments and onto the broad, sloping benchland of white sandstone that rims Sevenmile Canyon.

After closely paralleling the sloping canyon rim for about 1 mile, and skirting around a small red-hued tributary canyon, the trail climbs away from the rim. Beyond this point, the trail crosses the broad sand flats of Courthouse Pasture.

At each of the next several trail junctions, the correct route goes in the general direction of the massive Monitor & Merrimac buttes that dominate the scene, eventually to reach the solid slickrock terrace between the buttes. Some of the trail spurs encountered before reaching the buttes are worth exploring if time permits.

43

Uranium Arch, Monitor & Merrimac trail

From between the Monitor & Merrimac buttes there are several options, but the suggested route goes to the right around the base of Merrimac Butte, the larger of the two, then drops down to meet another graded trail near its northeastern tip.

Here, again, there are more options. A challenging side-loop trail that requires skillful driving goes left to the picturesque northwestern tip of Merrimac Butte, then follows an inconspicuous route completely around the butte at its base in a counterclockwise direction, to rejoin the main trail.

The graded trail to the north of the butte also continues west, eventually to join Utah 313, but one badly eroded grade makes this connecting trail hazardous, and virtually impassable when traveling toward the Monitor & Merrimac from Utah 313.

From the trail junction near the northeastern end of Merrimac Butte, the main route goes north through drift sand, then reaches another trail junction in about 1 mile. Here, it is possible to continue on down Mill Canyon and back out to U.S. 191. This spring-watered canyon is worth exploring, but the described route goes left here, toward a group of lofty spires. From the general vicinity of this junction it is possible to see a large arch high in the wall of the butte to the northeast.

The main trail goes quite near the tall spires, then continues on through broken terrain toward a huge gap in the western cliff line. A spur trail near the spires can be followed to go completely around them on their slickrock base.

44

Beyond the gap in the cliff line, the trail drops quickly into the main wash of Tusher Canyon, then on down this picturesque canyon. The spur trail up this canyon is worth exploring, if time permits.

Soon after the canyon finally opens out, the trail reaches another junction. Here, the left fork that climbs a hill of gray rubble is one approach to the Bartlett Wash trail, while the right fork heads eastward to close the big loop of the Monitor & Merrimac trail at the trail junction 1/2 mile from U.S. 191.

Notes:

1. Do not disturb the restored remains of the historic rock building near the beginning of this trail.

2. Warning: the first climb up the slickrock on the spur loop around Merrimac Butte is hazardously steep and sloping.

3. It is also possible to circumnavigate Monitor Butte.

4. An unusual type of agate can be found around the bases of the Monitor & Merrimac and the group of spires in Courthouse Pasture.

5. The Monitor & Merrimac buttes were named after those two Civil War ironclads because of their shapes, relative sizes and positions.

Determination Towers, Monitor & Merrimac trail

45

Trail Name: P O I S O N   S P I D E R   M E S A

Map: *Canyon Country* OFF-ROAD VEHICLE TRAIL MAP - Island Area

Time: 6 hours; 7 hours if the two spur trails are taken.

Type: Spur

Mileage: 18 miles round trip

Difficulty: moderate, with the trail surface largely packed or loose drift sand, wash sand and slickrock.

Access: this trail is a major and isolated spur off of Utah 279.

Trail Summary: this trail climbs onto a high, isolated slickrock mesa and offers many spectacular mesa-rim views of the Colorado River gorge, Moab-Spanish Valley and more distant panoramas in all directions.

Little Arch, Poison Spider Mesa trail

Rim view, Poison Spider Mesa trail

Trail Description:

This trail leaves Utah 279 about 6 miles downriver from the
U.S. 191-Utah 279 road junction. There, it goes through a gate
near the pullout where dinosaur track and petroglyph displays can
be viewed. The trail then ascends a series of switchbacks,
travels along a broad, sandy terrace and enters a narrow slickrock canyon to climb steeply upward toward the mesa top.

At about 3-1/2 miles from the trail start, it tops out onto
an expanse of slickrock where age-darkened mineral specimens lie
around on the sandstone. The trail here is confused, but goes in
a generally northeastward direction.

After about 1 mile on the mesa, the trail forks, with the
main trail going left, then climbing up onto a still higher,
relatively level sandy mesa. The trail travels this mesa for
about 1-1/2 miles, then drops down again.

A trail spur to the right appears about 2-1/2 miles from
where the trail first tops out, or about 6-1/2 miles from Utah
279. This spur goes about 1/4 mile to a viewpoint overlooking
the Colorado River gorge and the spectacular slickrock country of
Behind the Rocks beyond the gorge.

Less than 1/2 mile beyond this spur junction, another trail
fork appears. The right fork climbs slickrock and crosses sandy
stretches to end in about 1/2 mile, within a short walk of Little
Arch, a big natural span in the rivergorge upper rim that is
visible from Utah 279 far below, and Cane Creek Road on the
opposite side of the river.

The main trail goes left from the Little Arch spur junction,
and becomes difficult to find and follow for the next 2-1/2 miles
as it climbs through a labyrinthine mass of slickrock domes and
fins, sand dunes, washes and open sandstone terraces. If the
ultimate rim viewpoint is to be reached, considerable navigational skill will be needed along this stretch, especially
following precipitation that wipes out earlier tire tracks.

The trail goes generally northward, but twists and turns and
doubles back many times, before finally reaching the high northeastern rim of Poison Spider Mesa about 1-1/2 miles from The
Portal, where the Colorado River leaves Moab Valley, and directly
above where the river first reaches the base of the mesa.

47

The view here is magnificent, with all of Moab-Spanish Valley spread out below, the sand and slickrock wilderness of the Sand Flats and the southern part of Arches National Park beyond the valley, and the soaring La Sal Mountains and other highlands on the far horizon.

To the south and west, the lower slopes of Poison Spider Mesa and adjacent plateaulands are cut by the Colorado River gorge and its tributaries. From the end of a short spur trail that continues beyond the mesa rim overlook, the outline of Jeep Arch can be seen in a huge redrock outcropping to the northwest.

Notes:

1. There are other spurs along the Poison Spider Mesa trail. Some penetrate other scenic areas of the mesa, but most are mineral search trails that are not worth exploring.

2. Hikes along the rim of Poison Spider Mesa anywhere are quite rewarding.

3. There is a breathtaking view of Moab Valley and the river portal just a few yards northeast of Little Arch.

4. The first few hundred yards of the Little Arch spur trail travel solid slickrock and thus leave no tracks to follow.

5. As an aid to navigating the Poison Spider Mesa trails described, watch for small rock cairns, pieces of colored plastic ribbon fastened to trees, or other route markings.

6. Poison Spider Mesa is no more hazardous from venomous spiders than any other part of canyon country. For more details concerning the natural history of this region, see other volumes of the *Canyon Country* guidebook series.

Poison Spider Mesa trail

Trail Name: P O T A S H

Map: *Canyon Country* OFF-ROAD VEHICLE TRAIL MAP - **Island Area**

Time: 2 hours; 3 hours or more if one or both of the Pyramid Butte spur trails are explored.

Type: Connecting

Mileage: 15 miles; more if the spur trails are taken.

Difficulty: easy, with the trail surface largely graded, packed sediments.

Access: this trail connects the end of the pavement of Utah 279 with the White Rim trail.

Trail Summary: this trail provides a convenient connection between Utah 279 and the White Rim trail, but is worth traveling for the scenic beauty it offers as it wends its way past immense solar evaporation ponds, across colorful redrock desert and below lofty sandstone buttes.

Trail Description:

This highly scenic connecting trail continues beyond the end of the pavement, where Utah 279 ends at a potash refining plant beside the Colorado River. The trail parallels the river for about 1-1/4 miles to a boat launch ramp, then climbs abruptly up onto broad benchlands above the river, but still below the looming redrock buttes that dominate the setting on both sides of the river.

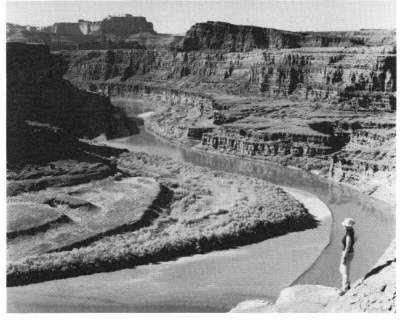

Pyramid Butte spur, Potash trail

49

After ascending past a series of curiously eroded red sandstone arroyos and a large balanced rock, the trail meanders past an immense expanse of shallow ponds, where solutions of potash and other minerals are concentrated by solar evaporation before refining.

About 5-3/4 miles from the trail start, a short spur trail to the right goes to Sallys Arch, a mid-sized but inconspicuous natural span in a low ridge of red sandstone.

As the trail leaves this area, it goes through a fence. About 1/2 mile beyond the fence, an inconspicuous spur trail angles left up a shallow wash. This spur heads toward the right side of the great redrock promontory called Pyramid Butte, to go counterclockwise around the butte. It ends at a spectacular rivergorge overlook, where the talus slopes of Pyramid Butte close the river gorge rim to further vehicle travel.

Less than 1/4 mile beyond where the first spur goes left, another one climbs a long, gentle slope, traveling generally southwestward toward the rim of a huge amphitheater that drains into the Colorado River gorge. The spur then continues close to the rim of that gorge for another 1/2 mile or so.

The main Potash trail continues beyond these spur trails through more beautifully eroded redrock desertland to closely parallel the rivergorge below Dead Horse Point, where an immense loop or "gooseneck" of the Colorado River can be seen far below. From there, the trail continues close to the gorge and at the base of a high butte, enters Canyonlands National Park, then climbs onto the White Rim, a gigantic terrace of light-colored sandstone.

There, the Potash trail joins the White Rim trail near the base of the Shafer Trail switchbacks.

Notes:

1. At several points along this trail, the gray limestone deposits contain ancient sea-life fossils.

2. Visitors to Dead Horse Point State Park can see part of this trail segment far below the point, but still high above the great river gooseneck that the point overlooks.

3. Watch for industrial traffic along the first 7 miles of this trail.

Evaporation ponds, Potash trail

Trail Name: R A I N B O W   R O C K S

Map: *Canyon Country* OFF-ROAD VEHICLE TRAIL MAP - Island Area

Time: 2 hours

Type: Connecting

Mileage: 6-1/2 miles

Difficulty: easy, with the trail surface largely loose or packed drift sand, wash sand or slickrock.

Access: this trail connects the Spring Canyon Point trail with the Levi Well trail near the Freckle Flat-Tenmile Wash trail junction.

Trail Summary: this trail travels a very colorful, eroded sandstone terrace below a picturesque redrock bluff, then travels rolling drift sand country and a shallow dry wash, with sheer-walled redrock buttes visible in all directions.

Trail Description:

The Rainbow Rocks trail branches right off of the Spring Canyon Point trail about 2-1/2 miles from the Dubinky Well Road at a prominence named "The Needles." This junction is at one end of a long, meandering bluff of colorfully banded sandstone called "Rainbow Rocks." The trail is confused at its beginning by intersecting mineral search trails, but keeps to the right to travel near the base of the sheer sandstone wall that begins at The Needles. The trail is sometimes difficult to find as it crosses stretches of slickrock in the first mile.

About 1-1/2 miles from the trail start, a short walk down a shallow watercourse in light-hued sandstone leads to a series of interesting potholes and a deep narrow grotto.

The trail then crosses a small canyon and continues on a picturesque rock terrace for another 3/4 mile before descending into rolling drift-sand country. Here, too, the trail is confusing, but heads generally northwestward, cutting off two large amphitheaters in the Rainbow Rocks butte, to drop into and travel down a major wash for 1/2 mile.

Springs and rock ledges soon bar further progress in the wash, but the trail leaves the wash to the right, to travel the rolling, eroded sediments along its bank. The trail joins the Levi Well trail between this shallow wash and the bluff base, as the bluff sharply changes direction to become the southern wall of Tenmile Wash.

Notes:

1. The Tenmile Wash-Freckle Flat-Levi Well trail junction is 1/2 mile west of the spring-watered wash near the Rainbow Rocks-Levi Well trail junction.

2. The white slickrock maze to the left of the first mile of this trail is interesting to explore on foot.

3. There are many curious sandstone erosional forms along the first 2 miles of this trail, and short hikes in both directions from the trail along this stretch are rewarding.

Rainbow Rocks

Trail Name: R E D   W A S H

Map: *Canyon Country* OFF-ROAD VEHICLE TRAIL MAP - **Island Area**

Time: 1 hour

Type: Connecting

Mileage: 6 miles

Difficulty: easy, with the trail surface largely packed drift sand or sediments, slickrock and some wash sand, with a little loose drift sand.

Access: this trail connects the Floy Wash Road with the Duma Point Road.

Trail Summary: this trail provides a convenient connection between two major access roads, but is also quite scenic as it winds through several miles of redrock desert and crosses an expanse of white slickrock that contains a deep and lovely gorge.

Trail Description:

  Beginning at the Duma Point Road about 6-1/2 miles from the Blue Hills Road, this trail angles to the right, then soon drops off of high ground onto the southern slopes of broad and shallow Red Wash. About 1-1/4 miles from the trail start, it crosses an expanse of white slickrock, and goes through a fence and some more slickrock before climbing out of the wash.
  Near the gate, the water course drops abruptly through a series of slides and potholes to enter a deep and narrow gorge. Beyond Red Wash, the trail meanders for several miles before going through another gate and then crossing White Wash. Just beyond White Wash, the trail joins the Floy Wash Road, about 3/4 mile from where that road ends at the Green River.

Trail Name: S A L T   W A S H

Map: *Canyon Country* OFF-ROAD VEHICLE TRAIL MAP - **Island Area**

Time: 1-1/2 hours; more if any of the many spurs are explored.

Type: Connecting (see Note 2)

Mileage: 9 miles

Difficulty: easy, with the trail surface largely packed sediments and some wash sand.

Access: this trail leaves the Floy Wash Road between its end at the Green River and its junction with the Blue Hills Road.

Trail Summary: this trail travels for several miles within Salt Wash, and offers colorful painted desert views and many spur trails along the way, to end at a viewpoint overlooking the Green River.

Trail Description:

The trail leaves the Floy Wash Road about 3 miles southwest of its junction with the Blue Hills Road. It travels down broad Salt Wash to the right of the wash bottom, with the surrounding terrain becoming more colorful with each mile. The trail closely parallels the wash bottom for about 6 miles, then climbs onto higher terraces, goes through a fence and ascends steeply out of the wash onto sand and slickrock highlands.

At about 8 miles from the trail start, it forks. The right fork is the southern end of the Crystal Geyser trail. The main Salt Wash trail goes left over a sharp, rocky ridge, then west down a sloping flat. It ends within a mile of the last trail fork, at a beautiful bluff-top viewpoint overlooking a wide bend of the Green River, about 1/2 mile upstream of where Salt Wash joins the river.

Notes:

1. The trail continues upriver beyond this overlook, but is badly eroded and descends through soft sediments that may make returning very difficult.

2. Although this 9-mile long trail is listed as "connecting," its last mile is a dead-end spur, for the reason indicated in Note 1.

3. There are several spur trails that branch from the Salt Wash trail at various places, some of which are worth exploring if time permits.

Trail Name: S E V E N M I L E C A N Y O N R I M

Map: *Canyon Country* OFF-ROAD VEHICLE TRAIL MAP – **Island Area**

Type: Spur; loop if optional connecting trail is taken.

Time: 6 hours if both branches of this trail are explored; still longer if the optional loop route is taken.

Mileage: 14 miles round trip to Arths Rim and back; longer if the spur to the lower canyon rimland is explored.

Difficulty: easy, with the trail surface largely packed drift sand or sediments and rough slickrock; difficult optional connecting trail.

Access: this trail is a major spur from the Gemini Bridges trail, but can also be reached via a 1-mile connecting spur from the Little Canyon Rim trail.

Trail Summary: this trail offers access to two stretches of the Sevenmile Canyon rim, and lofty Arths Rim with its spectacular panoramic views. The short optional trail connects to the Little Canyon Rim trail, making the two an excellent but challenging and demanding loop route.

Arths Rim, Sevenmile Canyon Rim trail

Trail Description:

     This trail angles left, or northeastward, from Arths Pasture Road about 3-3/4 miles from Utah 313. It first crosses gently sloping sand flats, then descends a sandstone ridge. About 2-1/2 miles from the trail start, a spur to the south connects with the Little Canyon Rim trail in about 1 mile.

     About 1 mile beyond this junction, an indistinct trail spur to the right leads to a series of trails that penetrate the redrock canyons visible to the east. Less than 1/2 mile farther on, the trail passes the end of the long ridge of sandstone it has been paralleling and comes to a trail fork.

     The left spur drops down a gradually descending series of wooded, slickrock-and-sand terraces, then heads upcanyon parallel to the south fork of Sevenmile Canyon. Several mineral search trails in this vicinity confuse navigation, but all are fairly short and offer various views of the interestingly eroded sandstone strata in this area, plus panoramic views to the north, across Sevenmile Canyon, of the Monitor & Merrimac buttes.

     From this junction, the trail to the right climbs, following a line of power poles. About 1/2 mile from the junction, the trail goes right at another fork, passing under and leaving the power lines. About 1/4 mile beyond this fork, the trail goes left at a faint junction, then starts a rough climb, to reach the high rim of Sevenmile Canyon about 1/2 mile beyond the lines.

     In another rough 1/2 mile, the trail reaches Arths Rim. From there, it continues closely parallel to the rim, passing the optional spur that connects it to the Little Canyon Rim trail in about 1/2 mile, and ending 1/2 mile beyond that. The views from along this mile of Arths Rim are spectacular.

Notes:

1. A short unmarked hike down the Little Canyon rimlands from the end of this trail goes to Lin-Lynn Arch, a large natural opening between two hanging canyons.

2. The optional connecting trail may be marked by a rock cairn.

3. Before driving more than 1/4 mile down the optional spur that connects this trail and the end of Little Canyon Rim trail, it is advisable to walk out the next 1/4 mile, to below where the spur descends a series of ledges and down through a steep and narrow drainage line.

Mirror Gulch, spur from Arths Rim to Little Canyon Rim trail

View from Arths Rim

Trail Name: S P R I N G   C A N Y O N

Map: *Canyon Country* OFF-ROAD VEHICLE TRAIL MAP - **Island Area**

Time: 10 hours if both branches of this trail are explored.

Type: Spur

Mileage: 55 miles round trip

Difficulty: easy, with the trail surface largely packed drift sand or sediments, with some slickrock.

Access: this trail spurs off of the Dubinky Well Road north of that road's junction with Utah 313.

Trail Summary: this spectacular trail offers breathtaking views of Spring Canyon and Bowknot Bend, and travels two long stretches within beautiful Labyrinth Canyon of the Green River.

Spring Canyon

Trail Description:

The trail turns left off of the Dubinky Well Road about 1-1/2 miles north of where that road leaves Utah 313. For the first 9 miles the trail crosses open sand flats, with slickrock domes and ridges to the north and with glimpses of Hellroaring Canyon to the south. There are several spur trails along this stretch that are worth exploring if time permits.

At a point about 4 miles from the trail start, a short hike down a drywash leads to a spectacular view of one spur of Hellroaring Canyon. Several miles farther on, the trail reaches the rim of a short spur of Spring Canyon and drops steeply into that deep and narrow sandstone gorge on a trail blasted from the canyon wall by early uranium prospectors.

Once it reaches the canyon floor, the trail continues toward the Green River past some of the springs that give the canyon its name. Near the canyon mouth, the trail branches, with one fork going upriver, the other downriver. At this fork, a cottonwood tree shelters the remains of an old, crudely built log cabin.

The upriver fork closely parallels the river below soaring cliffs, offering lovely, reflective views of the river and gorge walls. About 8 miles upriver, the trail reaches the mouth of Hey Joe Canyon, a short tributary of the Green River gorge, where the remains of earlier uranium mining activities stand beside the river. The trail then goes up Hey Joe Canyon for about 1/2 mile, to end at an abandoned mining settlement.

The downriver fork of this trail also closely parallels the river, but mostly on terraces somewhat above the water. The trail travels around Bowknot Bend, a great loop of the river. At one point, an old ore-bucket cable stretches across the river, and farther around the bend a series of mine shafts and some abandoned mining machinery can be seen on the opposite side of the river. Beyond this point, the rivergorge is largely unspoiled and primitive, just as Major John Wesley Powell and his exploring party first saw it in 1869.

The trail ends just upriver from the mouth of Horseshoe Canyon as it joins the main river gorge on the opposite side of the river about 7-1/2 miles from Spring Canyon.

Old log cabin, Spring Canyon trail

Notes:

1. The trail segments down into and beyond Spring Canyon are maintained only when the mines in the river gorge are active. At other times, they may be made difficult or impassable by erosion, fallen rock or dense vegetation growth along the river.

2. Some of the strata along the Green River and its tributary canyons offer good rock collecting.

3. The steep trail down into Spring Canyon can be hazardously slippery following precipitation.

Switchbacks, Spring Canyon trail

Spring Canyon Point

Trail Name: S P R I N G   C A N Y O N   P O I N T

Map: *Canyon Country* OFF-ROAD VEHICLE TRAIL MAP - **Island Area**

Time: 2 hours

Type: Spur

Mileage: 25 miles round trip

Difficulty: easy, with the trail surface largely packed sediments or drift sand and a little slickrock.

Access: this trail spurs off of the Dubinky Well Road near the windmill that marks the well.

Trail Summary: this trail crosses rolling sandflats country studded with sandstone outcroppings to go to the very tip of spectacular Spring Canyon Point, high above Labyrinth Canyon of the Green River.

Trail Description:

The trail heads west from the Dubinky Well Road a few hundred feet south of the windmill and about 6-1/2 miles north of where that road leaves Utah 313. For the first 2 miles the trail crosses rolling sandflats country, with the banded Rainbow Rocks slickrock ridge visible at the right.

Just beyond where the trail closely approaches the end of this ridge, the Rainbow Rocks trail forks right, but this trail continues in a westward direction. About 1-1/2 miles beyond the ridge, the Freckle Flat trail forks right at a directional sign.

The main trail continues through still more sandflats and slickrock country, angling southwestward beyond the Freckle Flat trail junction. About 2-1/2 miles from The Needles, or southernmost tip of the Rainbow Rocks ridge, a spur trail left goes toward small but interesting Juniper Arch in a low white sandstone outcropping, and on to the Secret Spire, a sandstone tower perched on the rim of one branch of Spring Canyon.

At 2-1/2 and 5 miles beyond this spur, the main trail goes through fencelines. About 1 mile beyond the second fence, and a short distance beyond a round, white dome of sandstone visible to the right of the trail, an interesting optional spur to the right goes toward Hey Joe Canyon. About 1/10th mile down this trail another spur goes right toward the base of the white dome.

The spur right is difficult to find and follow, but eventually rounds the upper end of Hey Joe Canyon, then continues to the rim of the Green River gorge, where the double Undine Bridges are visible across the river. In about 2 miles, the trail straight ahead reaches the rim of Hey Joe Canyon, near where it joins the Green River gorge. Spectacular Cliffhanger Bridge can be reached by a 1-mile hike along the river gorge rim.

About 10 miles from the main trail start, it travels out onto the elevated, slender peninsula of Spring Canyon Point. Along this stretch, tantalizing glimpses of the rivergorge rim can be seen at intervals in both directions.

The trail ends at the very tip of Spring Canyon Point. From this breathtaking overlook, the Green River can be seen more than 6500 feet below, sweeping in a sharp curve around the slender peninsula at the base of sheer sandstone cliffs. The upriver branch of the Spring Canyon trail can be seen far below, between the river and cliffs.

Notes:

1. About 1 mile back from the tip of Spring Canyon Point, a short hike south from the trail to the rivergorge rim offers a spectacular view across the narrow neck of Bowknot Bend.

2. Some of the several spur trails that leave the main trail along its middle stretches are worth exploring if time permits.

3. Rock collectors will find some interesting specimens near the tip of Spring Canyon Point.

Dubinky Well, Spring Canyon Point trail

Trail Name: T A Y L O R C A N Y O N R I M

Map: *Canyon Country* OFF-ROAD VEHICLE TRAIL MAP - **Island Area**

Time: 3 hours; 4 hours if the suggested hike is taken beyond the trail end.

Type: Spur

Mileage: 15 miles round trip

Difficulty: easy, with the trail surface largely packed or loose drift sand and some slickrock.

Access: this trail is an isolated spur off of the Island Road.

Trail Summary: this trail crosses open sandflats country near picturesque sandstone domes and ridges, to end near the tip of a lofty, slender peninsula that penetrates the spectacular Taylor Canyon system in the northern part of Canyonlands National Park.

Moses and Zeus spires, from Taylor Canyon Rim

Trail Description:

This trail branches west from the Island Road a little less than 3 miles south of the Utah 313-Island Road junction at The Knoll. For the first 2-1/2 miles the trail crosses open sand flats, where numerous mineral search trails checkerboard the otherwise unspoiled terrain. For about 1 mile of this stretch, the trail closely parallels a picturesque ridge of sandstone called Whitback Rock. At the southwestern end of this ridge, the trail descends to a lower level, goes between two interesting sandstone domes, then continues arrow-straight across the sand flats that lie just to the north of Taylor Canyon.

At about 5 miles from the trail start, it reaches the northern boundary of Canyonlands National Park. Drivers are cautioned to stay strictly on the trail beyond this point. For the last 1/2 mile before the trail ends on a slickrock point, short walks to the left lead to various rim viewpoints over-looking one branching spur of Taylor Canyon.

From where the vehicle trail ends, short hikes lead to spectacular viewpoints around the slender tip of a lofty peninsula that divides two Taylor Canyon spurs.

Hikers who go as far as possible out onto this tip will be able to view a row of enormous spires that continue beyond the tip. The largest of these, called "Moses," and a somewhat smaller one named "Zeus," have both been scaled many times in recent years by teams of "desert climbers."

Notes:

1. A few of the many spurs along the first half of this trail are worth exploring if time permits.

2. If this trail is closed at the National Park boundary, thus blocking vehicular access to the spectacular overlook at the trail end, it is still worthwhile hiking the rest of the way.

Taylor Canyon Rim and spires, aerial view

Trail Name: T E N M I L E   P O I N T

Map: *Canyon Country* OFF-ROAD VEHICLE TRAIL MAP - **Island Area**

Time: 2 hours; longer if the spur trail noted is explored.

Type: Spur

Mileage: 14 miles round trip

Difficulty: easy, with the trail surface largely packed sediments or drift sand and a little slickrock.

Access: this trail is a continuation of the Duma Point Road beyond its junction with the Red Wash trail.

Trail Summary: this trail provides access to the sand and slickrock country that rims upper Labyrinth Canyon of the Green River and the northern rimlands of spectacular Tenmile Canyon.

Tenmile Canyon, Tenmile Point trail

Trail Description:

The trail begins at the junction of the Duma Point Road and Red Wash trail and continues southwestward as an extension of the Duma Point Road. For the first 3-1/2 miles, the trail travels open sandflats terrain where numerous mineral search trails confuse navigation, but the main trail heads generally southwestward.

About 3-1/2 miles from the trail start, it turns toward the south. Just beyond this turn, the trail forks. The main trail goes left toward and past a corral at the base of a small sandstone bluff. About 2-1/4 miles beyond the corral, the trail reaches a spur to the left.

This left fork soon passes within a few yards of a large sandstone outcropping that has an arch on its north side. After about 1 mile, this spur ends at a drill site near a spectacular overlook into lower Tenmile Canyon, where several gooseneck loops of this deep, narrow gorge can be viewed from a rim projection just a few yards upcanyon from the drill site.

The main trail continues for about 1 mile in a generally southward direction, to end in a broad expanse of slickrock on a low rise of white sandstone.

A short hike beyond this rise in a southward direction leads to a rim overlooking an immense amphitheater that drains into the Green River gorge just upriver of the Tenmile-Green confluence.

Notes:

1. The entire Tenmile Point area is laced with mineral search trails, most of which go nowhere except to drill holes.

2. A 35-page booklet by Jack Bickers titled *"Biking, Hiking & 4-Wheeling* TENMILE CANYON," further describes recreational opportunities in and near this complex and beautiful canyon.

Tenmile Canyon, Tenmile Point trail

Trail Name: T E N M I L E   W A S H

Map: *Canyon Country* OFF-ROAD VEHICLE TRAIL MAP - **Island Area**

Time: 1/2 hour or less

Type: Connecting

Mileage: 2-1/2 miles

Difficulty: easy, with the trail surface largely packed sediments or drift sand, wash sand and a little slickrock.

Access: this trail connects the Duma Point Road with the Levi Well, Freckle Flat and Rainbow Rocks trails.

Trail Summary: this short trail segment serves as a convenient connection between an access road and three trails, but also offers points of interest along the way.

Trail Description:

The trail heads southeastward from the Duma Point Road about 5-1/2 miles from where that road leaves the Blue Hills Road. There may be a sign at the trail junction.

The trail first crosses open sandflats country, with massive sandstone outcroppings visible in all directions, then drops gradually through slickrock and drift sand terrain toward an open, shallow stretch of Tenmile Wash. Just before the wash, about 1-1/2 miles from the trail start, a right fork goes to a privately-owned cabin.

The main trail angles left to cross the wash, pass an old corral, then leave the wash. The trail then continues for about 1 mile, to connect with the Freckle Flat and Levi Well trails. About 1/2 mile east of this junction, the Levi Well trail crosses a spring-watered wash near several cottonwood trees. Just beyond this wash, the Rainbow Rocks trail comes in from the right.

Notes:

1. Tenmile Wash may be wet or have water in it at times, but is generally easy to cross except during actual flash flooding.

2. There is a dripping seep on a slickrock wall above Tenmile Wash just downstream from the trail crossing. A trough-and-bucket system catches this water for use.

3. Do not disturb the cabin or the water catchment at the nearby seep. Beware of the poison oak growing beneath the seep.

4. About 1/2 mile south of Tenmile Wash, a trail spur heads south from this trail. In about 1/2 mile, that spur trail forks. The left fork joins the Freckle Flat trail. The right fork continues south to enter a maze of mineral search trails, most of which go nowhere.

5. A 1/2-mile spur trail down Tenmile Wash from near the old corral ends at a delightful small waterfall and pool. Both may be dry during the summer season.

Stillwater Canyon, White Rim trail

"Ginpole" spur, White Rim trail

Trail Name: W H I T E   R I M

Map: *Canyon Country* OFF-ROAD VEHICLE TRAIL MAP - **Island Area**

Time: 2 or 3 days; longer if the various spurs are explored.

Type: Loop

Mileage: 85 miles

Difficulty: easy, with the trail surface largely packed sediments or drift sand, wash sand and slickrock.

Access: this loop trail as described connects at one end with Utah 313 and at the other end with the Island Road, a spur of Utah 313, but it also connects with the end of Utah 279 via the Potash trail.

Trail Summary: this trail begins on high plateaulands, descends to travel the spectacular White Rim benchlands below the Island-in-the-Sky of Canyonlands National Park, then climbs back onto the plateau, with outstanding scenic beauty visible from the trail along most of its length.

Shafer Trail switchbacks, White Rim trail

Trail Description:

This loop trail can be taken in either direction, but is described here going from east to west. The trail angles off of the Island Road at a point about 6 miles from that road's junction with Utah 313 at The Knoll, and about 1-1/2 miles north of The Neck within Canyonlands National Park.

The trail first descends from the plateau-top to travel a narrow terrace above the Shafer Canyon system. It then descends steeply down a breathtaking series of switchbacks called the "Shafer Trail," offering spectacular views to the east. At the bottom of this grade, the trail is joined on the left by the Potash trail coming from Utah 279, U.S. 191 and Moab.

The main trail goes right along the White Rim, which is clearly visible as a thick, hard layer of white sandstone. About 3 miles from the Potash trail junction, a short spur trail goes to Musselman Arch, a long, flat-topped span in the edge of the White Rim. Farther along, the immense silhouette of The Washerwoman can be seen standing on a high ridge that projects out from the Island-in-the-Sky butte.

Along the next stretch of trail, scenic beauty is everywhere as the trail roughly parallels the White Rim far below the Island-in-the-Sky, yet still high above the Colorado River and its complex of tributary canyons. At one point, a marked spur trail goes down Lathrop Canyon to the river, and a partly developed Park Service campground.

Farther along, the trail skirts fantastic Monument Basin with its many tall skyscraper-like towers and fins of dark red sandstone. Just beyond Monument Basin, the trail reaches a 2-mile spur that goes to the White Crack and another camping site.

The trail then rounds the southernmost tip of the Island-in-the-Sky and Junction Butte, a detached part of the Island. This point of the trail is very near to the geographic center of Canyonlands National Park.

Beyond Junction Butte, the trail heads generally northward, traveling along the western side of the Island-in-the-Sky and skirting several spectacular canyons and basins that are branches of the Green River gorge. Along this stretch, the trail crosses Murphy Hogback, an elevated ridge, then continues to skirt around still other Green River tributary canyons. In the vicinity of Queen Ann Bottom on the Green, a short spur trail goes to the river level at a stretch where the White Rim walls the river.

Beyond this junction, the main trail continues northward, drops down into a riverbottom, then climbs to cross a high ridge. At the summit of this ridge, a spur trail goes left to a viewpoint overlooking the ruins of a prehistoric Indian "fort" and a great loop in the river.

The main trail then descends to travel scenic riverbottoms, crosses Upheaval Canyon wash, then comes to the trail spur that enters Taylor Canyon. The trail into Taylor Canyon is often quite eroded and may be difficult to find and follow, depending upon recent runoff and usage.

About 2-1/2 miles beyond the Taylor Canyon trail junction, the main trail leaves Canyonlands National Park, and in another 4 miles comes to another trail junction. The left fork here continues up the Green River gorge as the Hellroaring Canyon trail. The main trail goes to the right and ascends a steep series of switchbacks up onto the high plateaulands, where it then travels 13 miles through rolling pinyon-juniper country to end at Utah 313 about 2-1/2 miles north of The Knoll and the Utah 313-Island Road junction.

Notes:

1. This entire trail, its several spurs and many of the major features along the way appear on a U.S. Geological Survey map of Canyonlands National Park and vicinity and on Park Service maps.

2. The National Park Service requires that vehicles taking the White Rim trail register at the Island-in-the-Sky ranger station before leaving.

3. The Park Service offers a small guide booklet that describes some of the White Rim trail highlights.

4. There are several primitive, undeveloped campsites designated along the White Rim trail for overnight use in addition to the partially developed campground at the lower end of Lathrop Canyon. Reservations are required for use of all established campsites along the trail. During the peak travel season, campsite reservations should be made well in advance.

5. It is not advisable to try driving this loop trail in one day. Two days are necessary if even the barest highlights are to be seen, and three days are desirable for full appreciation of this exceptionally beautiful area.

6. There are endless opportunities for short, spectacular hikes from the White Rim trail.

7. The "Shafer Trail" switchbacks can be viewed from developed overlooks at or near The Neck, where the Island-in-the-Sky joins the plateaulands farther north.

White Rim, aerial view

Trail Name: W H I T E   W A S H

Map: *Canyon Country* OFF-ROAD VEHICLE TRAIL MAP - Island Area

Time: Optional, depending on interest and vehicle capability.

Type: Spur

Mileage: optional.

Difficulty: easy in the sandy wash bottom, moderate on the slickrock domes but difficult in the sand dunes except with specially-equipped vehicles that are skillfully driven.

Access: this trail is a major spur off of the Floy Wash Road, not far from the Green River.

Trail Summary: this trail provides access to a labyrinth of slickrock canyons, a broad expanse of salmon-hued sand dunes and a huge ridge of colorful sandstone, where off-the-trail recreation is permissible.

Trail Description:

This "trail" is actually just a short stretch of sandy road that provides access into upper White Wash, where broad, sandy wash bottoms, sand dunes and slickrock combine to offer a variety of recreational opportunities to those with off-road vehicles.

The trail spurs south off of the Floy Wash Road about 7-1/2 miles southwest of the Floy Wash Road-Blue Hills Road junction, and about 3 miles northeast of the Green River. Driving toward the Green River, the trail goes left from the Floy Wash Road just a few hundred yards beyond an oil pumping installation on the ridge the road is traveling. As it descends from the ridge, the trail is confused by intersecting mineral search trails, but in general heads down into White Wash.

White Wash

In the wash, there are two options. One is to drive up the wash bottom and explore the interesting branching canyons of upper White Wash. There is a perennial spring in one branch.

The other option is open only to vehicles that are equipped for traveling soft dune-sand. From where the access trail first enters the bottom of White Wash, a spur trail climbs the far bank and enters a broad expanse of sand dunes, where dune-running and sand-hill climbing are permissible.

From the dunes, it is possible to climb up onto terraces on the great slickrock ridge beyond the dunes. By using these terraces, it is possible to go completely around the ridge, with panoramic views and interesting erosional forms along the way.

Near the south end of the main ridge, it is possible to cross a gap and climb onto still another slickrock mass, or to descend into the dunes. From the northeast part of the main ridge, it is possible to leave the slickrock, cross a dunes area and drop into one branch of the upper wash.

Notes:

1. Although the Red Wash trail crosses White Wash below this recreation area, a fence bars traveling directly up the wash.

2. Rock collectors will find interesting specimens near the wash downstream of the dunes area of White Wash.

3. The dune sand in the upper White Wash area can be very soft in the flat stretches between dunes. Vehicles not equipped with high-flotation tires can get trapped in such "dry quicksand."

4. Avoid damage to desert vegetation in the dunes area.

Cliffhanger Bridge, Spring Canyon Point trail spur

Jeep Arch, Gold Bar Rim trail spur

SUGGESTED
MULTI-SEGMENT ROUTES

Route Segments: Page

Bartlett Rim/Rainbow Rocks/Spring Canyon Point...... 75
Crystal Geyser/Salt Wash 76
Gemini Bridges/Four Arches Canyon/Long Canyon 76
Gold Bar Rim/Little Canyon/Bull Canyon 77
Sevenmile Canyon Rim/Little Canyon Rim 77
Long Canyon/Taylor Canyon Rim/Potash 78
Monitor & Merrimac/Bartlett Wash 78

NOTE:

The general directions for these sample one-day routes are
given starting and ending in Moab. For details, refer to the
trail segment descriptions. In addition to these multi-segment
routes, there are several single-segment trails in this area that
require one day or longer to explore, such as Poison Spider Mesa,
Spring Canyon, Hellroaring Canyon and the White Rim.

Segments: BARTLETT RIM/RAINBOW ROCKS/SPRING CANYON POINT

Suggested Route:

Drive north out of Moab on U.S. 191. Turn west on Utah 313,
then north on the Dubinky Well Road. About 4 miles after leaving
Utah 313, turn right onto the Bartlett Rim trail, exploring this
trail and its 1-mile spur. When this trail rejoins the Dubinky
Well Road, go south to just beyond the windmill, then west on the
Spring Canyon Point trail. About 2 miles from this junction,
turn right on the Rainbow Rocks trail. Where it joins the Levi
Well trail, turn left to the Freckle Flat trail, then left again
back to the Spring Canyon Point trail. At this junction, turn
right, or west, and continue on to Spring Canyon Point. Return
by the Spring Canyon Point trail all the way to the Dubinky Well
Road, then south on this road to Utah 313 and left, or east back
to U.S. 191 and on south to Moab.

Notes:

1. If less than a full day is available, bypass the Rainbow
Rocks-Freckle Flat trail segments.

2. This route offers good rock collecting at several points
along the way.

Segments: CRYSTAL GEYSER/SALT WASH

Suggested Route:

Drive north out of Moab on U.S. 191 to Crescent Junction, then west on Interstate 70. About 15 miles west of Crescent Junction, turn south on the Crystal Geyser trail. Continue on this trail to where it joins the Salt Wash trail. Turn right for 1 mile to the end of the Salt Wash trail, then return and travel southward on this trail all the way to its beginning at Floy Wash Road. There, turn left to Blue Hills Road, right to U.S. 191 and south to Moab.

Notes:

1. This route is long, but fairly fast and easy. It is not recommended during the warmer months, June through August.

2. The prime attractions along this route are good rock collecting, colorful painted desert formations and several views of the Green River before it enters deep Labyrinth Canyon.

Segments: GEMINI BRIDGES/FOUR ARCHES CANYON/LONG CANYON

Suggested Route:

Drive north out of Moab on U.S. 191 to where the Gemini Bridges trail leaves the highway about 7 miles north of the Colorado River bridge. Follow this trail, taking the short spurs to see The Bride and the tops of the Gemini Bridges. Continue on the main trail to the Four Arches spur trail and explore the main branch of this trail. Return to the Gemini Bridges trail, then continue west to Utah 313. There, turn left toward Dead Horse Point. About 2 miles beyond the Utah 313–Island Road junction at The Knoll, angle left onto the graded dirt Long Canyon trail. Stay on this trail, take the short spur at the head of the canyon, then go down the canyon to Utah 279. Turn left to go upriver on Utah 279 to U.S. 191, then south to Moab.

Notes:

1. If desired, this route can be traveled in the opposite direction, but the direction described offers better lighting for photographing the various highlights and panoramas along the way.

2. For a somewhat longer day, add the Bull Canyon spur trail to beneath the Gemini Bridges.

Segments: GOLD BAR RIM/LITTLE CANYON/BULL CANYON

Suggested Route:

Drive north out of Moab on U.S. 191 to where the Gemini Bridges trail leaves the highway about 7 miles north of the Colorado River bridge. Take this trail to its junction with the Gold Bar Rim trail in Little Canyon, then follow that trail to the rim where it ends. Return down the Gold Bar Rim trail to its junction with the Little Canyon connecting trail, then take that trail to its junction with the Bull Canyon trail. There, turn left to the trail fork in the Bull Canyon wash, explore the short spur down the wash, then explore the right fork to the Gemini Bridges. Return to the main Gemini Bridges trail, then turn right back to Little Canyon and on back to U.S. 191 and Moab.

Notes:

1. Although this route retraces part of the same trail on its return, the scenic beauty along the way will be different because of changed lighting.

2. If desired, the sequence of this route can be reversed to reach the Gemini Bridges first, when the morning lighting offers better photography.

Segments: SEVENMILE CANYON RIM/LITTLE CANYON RIM

Suggested Route:

Drive north out of Moab on U.S. 191, then up Sevenmile Canyon on Utah 313 to where the west end of Arths Pasture Road leaves this road. Take this road to where the Sevenmile Canyon Rim trail forks left, then take that trail to its end high on Arths Rim. There, find and take the short spur that connects to the upper end of the Little Canyon Rim trail, continue down that trail to where it rejoins the Gemini Bridges trail, then left into Little Canyon and on down to U.S. 191 and south to Moab.

Notes:

1. Explore the short spur that connects the upper ends of these two trail segments on foot before starting down, to make certain it is passable. This spur is rough, steep and difficult at best.

2. As an alternate return route, after returning to Arths Pasture Road, turn right to Utah 313, then left and down the Long Canyon trail to Utah 279 and upriver to U.S. 191.

Segments: LONG CANYON/TAYLOR CANYON RIM/POTASH

Suggested Route:

Drive north out of Moab on U.S. 191, then downriver on Utah 279. Just beyond Jughandle Arch, turn right up the Long Canyon trail. At the head of the canyon, take the short spur trail, then continue to Utah 313. Here, turn right and go to the Utah 313-Island Road junction, then turn left on the Island Road to its junction with the Taylor Canyon Rim Road. Take this spur trail to its end, then return to the Island Road, turn right to the head of the White Rim trail, where it starts down the Shafer Trail switchbacks. Go down this trail to the trail junction at the base of the grade, then turn left on the Potash trail. Stay on this trail to its Pyramid Butte spurs and, if time permits, explore at least one of these spurs. Return to the Potash trail and continue right to where it connects with Utah 279, then on upriver to U.S. 191 and Moab.

Notes:

1. This route can just as easily be taken in the opposite direction if desired. There are photographic advantages both ways.

2. This trail route can be supplemented with a highway trip out onto Dead Horse Point if time permits.

Segments: MONITOR & MERRIMAC/BARTLETT WASH

Suggested Route:

Drive north out of Moab on U.S. 191 to where the Monitor & Merrimac trail leaves the highway about 12-1/2 miles north of the Colorado River bridge. Turn left on this trail and drive it in the sequence described in its trail description, including, if desired, the loop spur around the Merrimac. As this trail leaves lower Tusher Canyon, turn left onto the Bartlett Wash trail and continue up the wash to where that trail connects with the Dubinky Well Road. Turn left on this road to Utah 313, then left to U.S. 191 and on south to Moab.

Notes:

1. If time permits, turn right on the Dubinky Well Road and take the Bartlett Rim loop trail before returning to Moab.

2. If time and the trail conditions permit an easy return, the spur trail into Hidden Canyon from Bartlett Wash can be added.

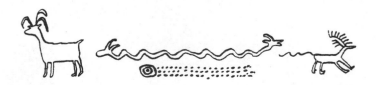

78

AUTHOR'S FAVORITE TRAILS

As an aid to canyon country visitors who have very limited time in which to explore this fascinating land, I have listed below my favorite trail segments in the Island Area. I made the selection on the basis of scenic beauty and variety, with only minor consideration given to the challenge of the trail. The choice was not easy, because every trail segment listed in this book has much to offer. In almost two decades of exploring southeastern Utah's backcountry, I have traveled every one of these trails, some many times, and have never failed each trip to see some aspect of beauty that I had missed before. That's the way it is in canyon country -- more beauty and variety than can possibly be seen, even in a lifetime.

> White Rim
> Monitor & Merrimac
> Poison Spider Mesa
> Gold Bar Rim
> Gemini Bridges
> Spring Canyon Point
> Sevenmile Canyon Rim
> Hidden Canyon Rim
> Long Canyon
> Rainbow Rocks
> White Wash

I hope this book adds to your enjoyment of canyon country exploring by off-road vehicle.

F. A. Barnes

FURTHER READING

Those who wish to know more about the unique and fascinating canyon country of southeastern Utah will find other books and maps in the *Canyon Country* series both useful and informative. They are stocked by many visitor centers and retail outlets in the region, or can be ordered through book stores.

The listed books are profusely illustrated with photographs, charts, graphs, maps and original artwork. The maps are also illustrated with representative photographs.

GENERAL INFORMATION

Canyon Country **HIGHWAY TOURING** by F. A. Barnes. A guide to the highways and roads in the region that can safely be traveled by highway vehicles, plus descriptions of all the national and state parks and monuments and other special areas in the region.

Canyon Country **EXPLORING** by F. A. Barnes. A brief history of early explorations, plus details concerning the administration of this vast area of public land and exploring the region today by land, air and water.

Canyon Country **CAMPING** by F. A. Barnes. A complete guide to all kinds of camping in the region, including highway pull-offs, developed public and commercial campgrounds, and backcountry camping from vehicles and backpacks.

Canyon Country **GEOLOGY** by F. A. Barnes. A summary of the unique geologic history of the region for the general reader, with a list of its unusual land-forms and a section on rock collecting.

Canyon Country **PREHISTORIC INDIANS** by Barnes & Pendleton. A detailed description of the region's two major prehistoric Indian cultures, with sections telling where to view their ruins, rock art and artifacts.

Canyon Country **PREHISTORIC ROCK ART** by F. A. Barnes. A comprehensive study of the mysterious prehistoric rock art found throughout the region, with a section listing places where it can be viewed.

Canyon Country **ARCHES & BRIDGES** by F. A. Barnes. A complete description of the unique natural arches, bridges and windows found throughout the region, with hundreds depicted.

UTAH CANYON COUNTRY by F. A. Barnes. An overview of the entire region's natural and human history, parks and monuments, and recreational opportunities, illustrated in full color.

CANYONLANDS NATIONAL PARK - *Early History & First Descriptions* by F. A. Barnes. A summary of the early history of this uniquely spectacular national park, including quotes from the journals of the first explorers to see and describe it.